Unsinkable Significance

Troy Ervin

Endorsements

A great read that reminds us that even when life breaks us, God's purpose does not, which makes our significance truly unsinkable.

Apostle Les Bowling

Pastor Troy Ervin is the greatest storyteller I know. The way he shares a story will make you laugh often, sometimes cry, when it's over you are left with something greater than just a story. In *Unsinkable Significance*, Pastor Troy does this in a powerful way. He shares his story, unlocks powerful truths found in Bible stories, and in the end helps each one of us come to a greater understanding of our own story. Every person on this planet wants to live a life of significance; we all want to make a difference. This book is a tool that will help you do just that!

Pastor Joshua Cossey
Faith Church
Oklahoma City, OK

There are many spiritual touch points in this book. The best part for me is the understanding and confirmation that regardless of your circumstances, past and/or present issues, God is there to love us, guide us and deliver us if we seek Him. Pastor Troy is a great storyteller and I love the humor he interjects from time to time. If your ax is broken, you'll find the fix. When you get to YOUR part, you'll know what I mean.

Tim Essex
Musician and Entrepreneur

Troy Ervin is one of the most positive people I know. His positive outlook does not arise from some pseudo-psychological feel-good pop theology. This book you hold in your hand is the product of God's work in His servant through days of brokenness and surrender. The author has experienced pain and heartache, but held firm to the Lord who says though weeping may last through the night, joy comes in the morning! It has been my privilege to know and serve, laugh, love and cry with Troy Ervin through friendship and ministry for almost forty years. He is a positive man because He trusts in the goodness of the Lord. *"He who did not spare His own Son, but delivered Him up for us all, how shall He not with Him also freely give us all things?"* (Romans 8:32 NKJV).

There is significance and meaning in your life and especially in the trial you're going through right now. Turn the pages of this book and be inspired to see how God turns disaster into a demonstration of His purpose in your life. Let God make your "iron swim." You can trust Him. Thank you, Troy, for sharing your heart and God's work in your life. To God be the glory!

Gary W. Heimbach
Assistant General Superintendent
Churches of Christ in Christian Union
Wheelersburg, OH

Everyone God created He creates for significance! Pastor Troy Ervin takes you through a biblical and personal look at the subject of significance. Then he applies the call of significance to your personal life. A must read for everyone.

Dr. James Horvath
Pastor of Calvary Lighthouse Church
Rochelle, IL

To the potential reader, I ask: What is the definition of "significance"? What does it mean to you? To God? What drives a man or woman to spiritual greatness? Could it be the innate desire to leave a legacy for generations to come? The desire to simply say, "I was here"?

In this heartfelt, scripture-focused book, Pastor Troy Ervin brings an understanding of deep-rooted truths hidden in the hearts of man since our Creator first walked with man in the garden. This understanding is THE key that unlocks the answers to the greatest questions on earth, "Why am I here and what is my purpose?"

Pastor Troy proves the point that, one way or another, we all leave a legacy. What legacy will you leave? Will it be a legacy of your own thoughts and making, based on earthly rewards where everyone knows your name? Or, will your legacy be rooted in Surrender (To God), Brokenness (In Him), and the accomplishment of the greatest calling ever given to man? To roll back the veil and let others see Christ for who He really is!

In this writing you will, through the use of personal life and family stories, timely quotes and practical application, see the doors open to YOUR destiny, seeing what God sees IN you and FOR you; bringing insight and understanding about how we are influenced and how we influence others, leaving a legacy for generations to come.

It is my honor to highly recommend this book to those who have not yet met their Savior, the new in Christ, and to the seasoned believer as well. This is a book to reread and pass on to generations to come!

Bishop Dr. Jeffrey W. Larson, DM
Fort Worth, TX

Last year over one million people bought drills. The truth is, not a single one of them wanted a drill. What they wanted was a hole.

Similarly, each of us is searching for significance. But what we don't realize is that it's not found where we expect it. Instead, it's discovered in a most unusual place, brokenness. Troy Ervin's excellent book, *Unsinkable Significance*, will help you understand "why you are here" from a profoundly unique perspective found in a rarely told story about a stick in the Bible. This book touched me so deeply that I have a small branch from a tree sitting on my desk as a reminder of God's truth from this book.

I had the honor of working with Troy from when this book was just an idea through to the final manuscript. He poured his heart into this life-changing message. Full of captivating stories and practical examples, this book will not leave you the way it found you. It will compel you to live your life, from this day forward, in a way that matters. I highly recommend it.

John Mason
Author of the best-selling book, *An Enemy Called Average,*
and numerous other best sellers

Read and you will be entertained, informed, and inspired! Most of all reminded that you are truly significant and that God's purpose for you is always within reach.

Charles Walters
Domestic and International Evangelist

Dedication

One of the many reasons I felt compelled to write this book is my four children. They are, without a doubt, four of the greatest blessings God has given me in this life.

As much as I have had a burning desire to find God's will and my significance in life, the passion in me for them to know their purpose is even greater.

To Katie, my oldest, who is so much like me, yet different enough to be so much better! Her heart and passion for life and ability in friendship will take her to great heights.

To Alex, an awesome young man, whose athleticism is great, but his good heart and ability to love are even greater.

To Bella, who will set her mind to something and keep going until it is finished, and who will capture you in such a way as to enlist you in her project.

To Baylee, who comes in like a tornado, but when she's gone, you miss the wind.

Although I pray this book will help an untold number of people to follow Christ and to walk in significance, I wrote it with four people in mind: Katie, Alex, Bella, and Baylee.

I dedicate this book to you and pray that you will always realize God created you on purpose and with purpose. Remember, you truly can do all things through Christ who strengthens you! I love you more than breath!

—Dad

Contents

Foreword

Marvin Gaye asked in a song, "What's goin' on?" The Who sang the question, "Who are you?" Frank Sinatra crooned defiantly, "I did it my way." It seems everybody is in search of meaning.

On the campus of the Ivy League Dartmouth College, a group of students and alumni embarked on a mission to intellectually and spiritually pursue truth. They believe that faith in God and reason can be integrated into everyday life. From that premise they created the Eleazar Wheelock Society. The group's purpose is to engage the world with godly wisdom to inform and enrich each other.

As an invited guest to the organization's 2018 conference, I was asked to provide my professional observations as a journalist for a leading news organization and my personal thoughts and reason for my faith in God. The organization chose a striking theme for its conference: What Is Your Why? To further define the point of the event, the students used a quote from the famous British author, Lewis Carroll, who wrote; "If you don't know where you're going, any road will take you there."

The very idea that students on the campus of one of the top colleges in the country are seeking godly wisdom to understand why they exist is encouraging. It is evidence that all of us throughout the world have a burning desire to know why we exist. Who are we? What are we here for? Where are we going? When and how will we get there?

Mankind is thirsty and hungry for knowledge. We are in a constant pursuit of value and meaning. In his book, *Unsinkable Significance,* Troy Ervin brilliantly and emotionally merges knowledge and wisdom, reason and faith to provide answers to the questions you have about your very existence.

I know Troy Ervin. He is a husband, father, pastor, businessman, musician, basketball player, coach, and avid runner. Wherever Troy goes, he takes time out to first pray and stay close to God. Then he puts on his running shoes and runs for five miles. Troy will tell you that he is running for God. In fact, in this book, he is chasing after God in a desperate pursuit to satisfy his own hunger and thirst to find himself and his value in the heart and hands of a loving God. Like the students and alumni at Dartmouth's Eleazar Wheelock Society, Troy is asking the right question, intellectually and faithfully, that all of us are asking: Why?

As you read this book you will learn that God wants to embrace and engage humanity with His divinity. You will discover that Troy is a God Chaser who understands that our search for significance is found in the Bible where all kinds of people, rich and poor, bruised and broken, ultimately find healing and purpose in God. Your takeaway from this book is that you will be inspired and you will even know why you are here. You will learn that through God's love all of us can have *Unsinkable Significance.*

Kelly Wright
Journalist
America's Hope News

Introduction

Why Am I Here?

We are all born asking questions. We ask how to find success. How do I get from where I am now to where I want to be? Where do I go? What do I do? But the biggest question of all . . . the question we have all asked ourselves at one time or another is, "Why am I here?"

Everybody asks the big WHY question at some point in their lives. What is my purpose? Why was I born and put on this earth? The truth is that God created all of us on purpose and with a purpose. But many of us struggle to discover what that purpose is. Most of humanity lives aimless lives, drifting about trying to figure out what their ultimate goal in life is. They want to know where they fit.

In short, it's a search for significance. This desire for significance, to know that our lives will count for something, is embedded deep within us. It's knitted into the very fabric of our being, built in from the day we were conceived. We all have a dream within us, a desire to be known, to be remembered for something significant.

In my case, I knew early on as a child that there was a calling for significance on my life. But there was a particular moment when that ethereal feeling crystalized and became very real and very specific.

A Moment at Camp Meeting

I was about fifteen years old, and I was attending a camp meeting with my parents at a Holiness camp called Wellston Camp. Now you've got to understand, these were the days of the old camp meetings. They've almost died away these days but back then, these precious times in the heat of the summer were the high points of my year.

The camp was on a beautiful piece of property just outside the city in rural Ohio. There were cabins and places to camp, but everything revolved around the considerable tabernacle that was in the center of it all. The tabernacle was an open-air wooden structure with a stage at the front and benches and pews set on a sawdust floor throughout.

Each evening after supper we'd gather in the tabernacle for services. Huge crowds would convene, 1,500 people, maybe more would endure sweltering heat as we jumped and shouted and praised the Lord with all our might. And then, after worship, the handheld fans would come out and we'd settle in for the preaching of the Word.

On this night, I believe the preacher was a man named John Coffee. Coffee was quite an orator and a gifted preacher. Ignoring the heat, we sat, leaning forward in the pews with rapt attention, hanging on his every word. I can remember him stretching his arm out over the crowd and talking about God carpeting the earth with the green grass and tacking it down with the wild growing daisies. We soared to the heights, carried aloft by his words. I don't remember what his text was that night, nor the subject of his sermon but what is stamped on my brain and what I'll remember until the day I die is the backdrop behind him as he preached.

I Want to Be What You Want Me to Be

The tabernacle was open behind the stage, and from my vantage point, I could see outside, clear to the horizon. The sun was setting. The silver sheen was turning to soft gold, and soon it lit up the heavens with a brilliant fiery red. And it was in that moment, as the sun was taking its plunge below the horizon, that I remember sensing the enormity of God . . . and just how small I was in comparison.

But at the same time, inside me, there was this massive desire not only to serve Him but to serve Him in a significant way, to make every breath honestly count. A declaration was rising in my spirit. I wanted to be someone of value to Him and His Kingdom, and to others. When John Coffee was finished preaching, I remember him giving an altar call. He wanted us to take some sort of action. I don't know whether I made my way down that sawdust aisle or not, but I do know that I had a meaningful exchange with God the Father, sitting on my bench at the back of that sweltering tabernacle, wanting Him to take over my life. I told Him, "I want to be whatever it is You want me to be. No matter what. I want to give You control, to let go and let You have my life."

It was a wonderful defining moment in my life. But of course, I was just a teenager, immature in the ways of the Lord and the next couple of years, I struggled. I wrestled with God, as we all do, trying to make sense of my life, trying to find my purpose.

But when I turned eighteen, I finally was able to settle the turmoil and answer the question about my path of life. I had an inward assurance that I was called to preach the Gospel. I wanted to be like A. B. Maloy, who was my pastor growing up, like Don Pfeifer and John Coffee, and so many others along the way who had influenced my life by their powerful preaching. I wanted to be like them, to someday stand in front of a crowd of people and preach the Gospel.

In the Pulpit

Once I settled the matter, it didn't take long for an opportunity to come knocking. Before I turned nineteen years old, I had preached my first sermon. I remember it was at a little church in Wellston, Ohio, just off of Mulga Road called The Zion Number Three Church. I'm not sure where Number One or Number Two were, but this church was Zion Number Three! They knew of the "Ervin boy" and they called and asked me to preach. I agreed to it, even though I had never preached in front of anybody, didn't even know what I was doing. All I had was the assurance of my calling from the Lord.

I preached from Matthew chapter 28 verses 18-20, "All power is given unto me in heaven and earth. Go ye therefore, and teach all nations, baptizing them in the name of the Father, and of the Son, and of the Holy Ghost: Teaching them to observe all things whatsoever I have commanded you: and, lo, I am with you always, even unto the end of the world. Amen." That was the first text I ever preached, and after I had finished, I remember thinking that I did all right.

Next, I was asked to preach at a little Freewill Baptist church, just there by the tennis courts in Wellston on one of the back streets. It was a Sunday evening; there may have been fifteen people there. I preached from John chapter 9 about the blind man. I was hoping to improve over my first time out, but instead, I was worse. Much worse!

My confidence had been taking a beating from the enemy, and I once again wrestled with whether or not I was even called to preach. I had prepared enough material to preach for at least thirty minutes, but by the time I'd reached the three-minute mark, I had no more left, I was done. It was horrible. And when I tell you it was awful, that's precisely what I mean. It was really bad! It was so bad in fact that as I stepped down from the pulpit, I knew that I never wanted to preach again. I'm sure if you asked those fifteen folks who heard me preach, they'd probably tell you that they never wanted me to preach again either! I was still uncertain about my calling and not fully committed to it. I wasn't "all in," and that's why I did so poorly. I left the church convinced that I was done. No more preaching for me.

That night when I got in my car, I was so upset that I couldn't even go straight home. I was restless and miserable, trying to sort things out. I drove around town in my little old 1981 five-speed Toyota Celica. I drove down street after street and road after road. I wept and cried out to God, "Lord, I want to be significant and I want to serve You. But this obviously isn't the right thing for me to do. I did so poorly . . . and for so few people. I'm just glad it wasn't a big crowd! This just isn't going to work."

As I continued to drive around town one thought continued to roll over and over again in my head, "This isn't going to work." At about 1:00 in the morning I finally rolled up to a little stop sign just a block or two from my house, not far from a closed down factory. It was dark and deserted, and the old factory across the street reflected the way I felt, useless and abandoned.

I just sat there in my car in a daze. My hopelessness had exhausted me; I was drained and felt I didn't even have the strength to make it the rest of the way home. I had prayed all the words I knew to pray. I had wept all the tears I had to cry. I was at the end of myself and didn't know what else to do. I didn't have the answers I so desperately needed.

My nephew, Rob, who is like a brother to me, pulled up next to me in his car and rolled down his window. He said, "Troy! We've been looking everywhere for you! Everyone's worried sick. We couldn't find you."

Rob had already been preaching for a couple of years and when I looked at him and said, "It was awful," he replied, "Yeah. It sure was!" I lashed out at him, "Get out of here and leave me alone!"

But before following him to my house, I remember making a declaration to the Lord. I looked out through the windshield into the darkness from the loneliness of my little old car and said, "God, I admit, I don't know how to do this. All I'm doing is making a fool of myself." Then, right in the front seat of my car on that dark night I finally came to the place where I could lift my hands in complete and utter surrender. I said, "Lord. All right. I yield. If for the rest of my life, every time I'm given the opportunity to preach and make a fool of myself, then I promise . . . I'll be Your fool."

For me, that was my moment. That was the moment everything changed. After I uttered those words, the light of the Lord came into that car and into my spirit. His anointing began to flow through me. From that moment on, preaching was the most natural thing on earth to me. I had found my significance in Him.

From Brokenness to Significance

I believe that brokenness is the gateway to surrender. And surrender is the only real way to find significance in this life. When I say surrender,

I mean giving up trying to do things our way, in our own time. Surrender is that moment where you can genuinely come to a place of death and say, "Lord, I'm Yours." It's like a seed planted in the earth. Before it can ever bear fruit, it has to die. It has to fall to the ground and give up being a seed.

Much of humanity can boast about being a proud seed. "We have so much potential! Whatever our minds can conceive, we can achieve!" And while that may make a nice bumper sticker, it's not true without first brokenness and then surrender. Like seeds lined up on a table, they will always be seeds until they are placed in the ground to die.

It's that process of falling to the earth and dying where the power of transformation is unleashed. Think about the time Christ spent in the garden the night He was arrested. He had come to the crossroads where His purpose in life was to be revealed and He had a decision to make. Would He insist on His way and run for the hills to escape capture or would He surrender and yield to the will of His Father? Out of the abundance of His heart, His mouth whispered in the darkness, "Not My will but Your will be done." His brokenness led Him to the garden to pray. His prayers led Him to ultimate surrender. And His surrender led Him to the significance of the Cross, which was His purpose on this earth.

Think about other examples you may know from the Bible. Jonah didn't fulfill his mission to preach in Nineveh until he found brokenness in the belly of the whale. Moses didn't find significance leading the Hebrews out of Egypt until he'd surrendered on the far side of the desert. Paul didn't write one word of the New Testament or plant one church until he'd surrendered that day on the road to Damascus. Even the prodigal son didn't return home to his father until he had "come to himself" (Luke 15:17) in the midst of the pigpen. The process of brokenness leading to surrender and surrender leading to significance is repeated over and over again throughout the pages of history. That's the way of the Kingdom, the way God works in all of us.

Finding significance in life is not easy, and there are no shortcuts. It's a process that begins with brokenness. I've counseled hundreds of people, maybe even thousands over the years who have been on a quest for significance with no success. In most cases, it's because they hadn't arrived at the place of brokenness. They hadn't yet "fallen to the earth." There was no surrender. Like in my case, they hadn't yet gotten to the place where they could lift their hands in surrender and say, "Lord, I'm done."

Crisis Moments

I believe in the power of those crisis moments that bring us to brokenness. Like my dark night of the soul in the car, I wouldn't have come to that place of surrender without first hitting rock bottom. And without surrender, I would have never found the path to true significance in my life. And isn't that what the New Birth is? Dying to our old selves and being born again . . . a whole new creation.

A crisis moment is a moment of impact. It's an instant where—BAM—something happens to you and causes everything to change in an instant. Like the bolt of lightning that knocked Saul from his horse, a crisis moment is a flash in time. But life isn't lived in crisis moments. Life is lived day to day and year to year, and real significance isn't found in a flash but rather over a lifetime of surrender. Significance is found in the ebb and flow of brokenness and surrender.

You may find yourself at the low point of brokenness. Your search for significance may have brought you to an intense moment of crisis. But that doesn't mean that you've reached the end, it doesn't mean that your search is over! Be encouraged! You are not done and God is not finished with you yet!

You are redeemable no matter what you may have done and no matter how far you may have fallen. Believe me, I've been there. I've messed things up in my own life from time to time and had to find God in the midst of my brokenness. But I've learned that no matter how bad we've messed things up, we are redeemable. God isn't finished with us yet!

1

I Was Here—Our Desire for Significance

I've always loved a particular story from the Old Testament of the Bible. It's a story most folks are familiar with since the days of Vacation Bible School. It's a story mostly told for the miraculous event of the prophet making an iron ax head float. But I believe there's so much more to this event, so much more for us to learn about the human heart and its yearning for purpose and significance.

For me, there's layer upon exciting layer of profound content in this short passage. So much so, it's been the basis for several of my sermons and now . . . this book.

> *And the sons of the prophets said to Elisha, "See now, the place where we dwell with you is too small for us. Please, let us go to the Jordan, and let every man take a beam from there, and let us make there a place where we may dwell."*
>
> *So he answered, "Go."*
>
> *Then one said, "Please consent to go with your servants."*
>
> *And he answered, "I will go." So he went with them. And when they came to the Jordan, they cut down trees. But as one was cutting down a tree, the iron ax head fell into the water; and he cried out and said, "Alas, master! For it was borrowed."*

So the man of God said, "Where did it fall?" And he showed him the place. So he cut off a stick, and threw it in there; he made the iron float. Therefore he said, "Pick it up for yourself." So he reached out his hand and took it.

2 Kings 6:1-7 NKJV

Stepping Into Purpose

This is the story of a young man who had enrolled in Elisha's "School of Prophecy." He wanted to be part of something new, something exciting, something bigger than just himself. So he enrolled in the school and became a disciple of the prophet.

Now the school had many students just like this young man. We don't know exactly how many but we do know there were at least fifty "sons of the prophets" in the school. The school had grown, and now they were busting at the seams, outgrowing their building. The students went to Elisha and asked if they could go down to the river and cut down trees to make a bigger place to meet. Elisha gave them permission and agreed to go to the river with them to help oversee the project.

So, they all went down to the Jordan River and proceeded to get to work cutting down trees and preparing them for use in building the new structure. I can imagine the energy of the young men as they began to work. This was a big project, a new venture. They were going to get a new building! And not only that, they were going to build it themselves. What pride they must've felt. How excited they must have been as they split up into work crews with some cutting down trees, some stripping off limbs and bark, and others digging a foundation for the new structure.

It just so happens that in this story, the young man eagerly volunteered to be a part of this exciting new project. He steps up to be included. He wants to do something significant with his life. He's looking for purpose, looking for a cause to pour himself into.

So he quickly borrows an ax from a fellow student and makes his way down to the river with the other students. He finds a good tree to start cutting down, a tree that is straight and strong and begins to swing his borrowed ax.

Now I believe this borrowed ax probably wasn't in the best shape. It probably wasn't too sharp. Maybe it was rusty and the ax head was a bit wobbly. The owner of the old ax might have even had a newer one . . . that's why he was able to lend out his old one.

The Ax Head Is Lost

So, this student begins to work with this wobbly, dull ax, doing his best to cut down trees and be a productive member of the team. Who knows how many times he had to work on that borrowed ax trying to file down the edge or beat the wobbly ax head back securely on the ax handle.

I imagine the student working on cutting down his first tree. The sweat is glistening on his bare back and rolling down his forehead. He's so focused on his work he doesn't even notice that the ax head is slipping up the handle farther and farther, until all at once on a mighty back swing, the ax head goes flying off the handle and out into the river!

Immediately the student cries out. The prophet Elisha is close by and the student pleads with him, "Oh no! Please help me get the ax head back . . . I borrowed the ax, it doesn't belong to me!"

The students had heard the commotion, and they all stopped what they were doing and gathered around, leaning in to see what the prophet was going to do. Elisha has compassion on the young man and wants to help. He asks him, "Show me where in the river it landed." The student pointed to a spot in the water where he saw the ax head sink.

I imagine Elisha pausing and taking a breath as if trying to decide what to do next. Then moving quickly as if he'd made up his mind, he did something unexpected. He didn't call down fire from heaven, and he didn't begin to declare what he wanted with a loud voice. He merely cut a stick from a nearby tree and threw it in the river. How strange that must've seemed to the students still gathered around. They were used to seeing the prophet do mighty things under the power of the Lord. But this? How was throwing a worthless stick in the water going to help the poor guy get his borrowed ax back?

The Iron Did Swim

Elisha continued to stare at the water's surface. Others along the river-bank followed his gaze and watched the stick float effortlessly on the water. Soon, the surface of the water began to move. Something was happening. Now the water bubbled and grew choppy as if a mighty school of fish was feeding. Suddenly, the ax head appeared on the surface of the water, right where the stick had landed! I love the way it's worded in the *King James Version*, "the iron did swim." What once was lost was now found. The iron did swim!

And not only did the ax head begin to float, but it also began to drift closer to the river's edge. When it got close to the bank, Elisha smiled and looked at the stunned young man. He pointed to the ax head and said, "Reach in and grab it." And that's what the young man did. The ax head was returned, and the young man was able to continue his work.

There's so much in this story about the desire for significance, wanting to be chosen for something, even the anonymity of the young man. There's the wobbly ax head and the compassion of the prophet to help the young man in need. There's the miraculous power of a loving God doing the impossible, moved by the desperation of the young man.

This story means a lot to me. It reveals something fundamental about the human heart and its desire to be recognized. But the story also shows God's desire to share His significance with us . . . to put us into places where we can find fulfillment through purpose, through the pursuit of a cause.

I had been meditating on this story for a while when I encountered something profound on a walk in the woods. God revealed something to me that sheds a whole new light on what drives us to do the things we do.

I Was Here

It was several years ago now that I went on a walk in the woods while on a trip home to see my mom. In those last few years of my mother's life, I made a special effort to get back at least once a week for a visit. On this particular trip, I remember it was the fall of the year, a beautiful day. We were sitting together in the house talking, and during a lull in the conversation, I felt the tug to get outside. I told my mom, "I think I want to go out and take a walk."

Now she lived just right on the edge of Wellston, Ohio. The house was on New Hampshire Avenue, just up on a little knoll. The street continued on past mom's house for a bit and then dead-ended right at the woods. So, I strapped up the laces of my hiking boots, threw my jacket over my shoulder and walked to the end of mom's street and stepped off into the woods.

As I said, it was a beautiful fall day; there was a brisk feel in the air, the sun was brilliant in the heavens, and the trees had just started to change color. When I was a child, I used to say that it was as if God had come down with His paintbrush and painted all the leaves different colors. It was simply breathtaking to stand on the side of that mountain, there in the place where I grew up in southeast Ohio, a place I knew so well. I could look across the ravines and the valleys and see the gorgeous handiwork of our Heavenly Father. It was beautiful. I just wanted to spend a little time with the Lord and be alone, and this was the perfect place to do it.

As I was walking through the woods, I came upon a massive old tree. From the gnarled roots that anchored the enormous trunk to the ground to the tips of the branches that reached to the heavens, this tree was huge. I stopped to take notice and almost walked on when I happened to see, carved into the bark of that old tree was a man's name. I didn't know the man, but I recognized the family name. I had no idea how long the carving had been there. It was impossible to tell just by looking, but I could tell it had been there a while.

His name was crudely carved into the bark, probably with a pocket-knife, the kind we all used to carry in our pockets when we were boys. I stepped up to the tree for a closer look and ran my fingers over the rough edges of each letter. It was then that I saw that underneath the name something else was carved. In the very same crude stroke, three additional words were etched into the bark, "I was here."

The words were simple, but as I continued to think about it, their meaning took on a profound implication that I will never forget. I walked away from that tree with this whole idea that there's something deep within the human spirit that yearns for significance. Something that cries out, "I was here. I breathe. I exist. I'm somebody. I was here!"

Much like the story of the young man with the ax, he wanted to be more, to do more than he was doing. He stepped up and enrolled in that school and volunteered to work on that project. He wanted everyone to know, "I am here."

We see this theme of a search for significance everywhere we turn from popular music to movies to television, even to advertising. There's no mistaking that the message of recognition and significance resonates deep within the heart of humanity.

A Deep Down Desire

Since that day in the woods, I've asked myself, "Where does this desire come from? What's at the root of it?" It's become evident to me that this desire comes from our Creator. He made us and knows us . . . even the number of hairs on our heads, so it would make sense that He knit this yearning for significance within our DNA.

We can see this desire as it leaps off the pages of holy script. It's a fire in the soul, a deep-down yearning. We see it in the life of Abraham as he walked up the side of the mountain with a dagger in his hand and his son at his side. He was driven up that rugged mountain trail by the word of the Lord and the desire for significance.

Or what about Noah, who had spent 120 years crying out for righteousness' sake with not even one convert and then had to force his own family into the ark to be saved. What was his driving force? Those three simple, yet haunting words, "I was here."

Joseph will follow a dream all the way from a pit in the desert to the very throne room of Egypt with the praises of men echoing in his ears and the words "I was here" echoing in his heart.

There was Moses who had a desire to free his people and David tending the flock on the backside of the hill. Rahab who hid the spies and Esther who felt like she'd married the king for such a time as this. There was Daniel who faced Jerusalem and prayed three times every single day even though he was held hostage in a foreign land; and let's not forget the three Hebrew boys who survived a fiery furnace all because they were urged onward by the words, "I was here."

There was Peter who left his nets and followed Christ for three years and Paul who wrote two-thirds of the New Testament. On and on and on, these examples, and so many others from scripture cry out, "I am here!"

I was thinking about this all the way home from the woods, and it's been stuck in my mind since I took that hike and saw the carving in that tree. I thought of the people in the Bible, including the young man from the story in 2 Kings 6. The more I thought about it, the more I was reminded even of my own children and their desire for some notice or acknowledgment. From their hearts, they cry out, "Watch me, Daddy!"

From my oldest, Katie, who says, "Daddy, are you going to make it to my volleyball game?" "Oh, I'll be there, baby." Or my son, Alex, saying, "You're not going to miss my football game, are you?" "Oh no, son. I'll make it. I wouldn't miss it for anything."

Or Bella, who wants to play soccer, but is incredibly artistic as well. She's always working on one project or another. A while back, on a speaking trip, I found something in my suitcase that she'd made me when she was only three or four years old. On it, she'd written a message and spelled "daddy" D-A-D-E-Y. It probably wouldn't mean much to most people, but I saw it for what it was . . . an expression of love, a desire to be noticed. It was precious to me.

Then, of course, there's my youngest, Baylee, who wants you to see everything she does. She wants you to acknowledge her. Over the years I've probably witnessed over a million of her cartwheels. I especially remember the one where she got too close to the table and my plate of spaghetti ended up all over the floor in the kitchen!

Significance and Purpose

What's behind all that? What is that desire we all carry? I'm here. Watch me. Notice me. There's something in all of us, even if we don't have a relationship with God, there's something in each of us that wants someone out there to watch us, to acknowledge that we exist, to notice that we are here.

My kids, who are cast in my image, want me to notice that they carry my voice, my fingerprints, my talent, my personality, my uniqueness, my footprint. Just like we all do with God. We are His handiwork, cast in His image and we want Him to see Himself in us. We are designed for destiny, prepared for a purpose, and created for a cause.

Author and speaker John Mason says, "You're born an original, don't die a copy!" I love that because it speaks to this very idea of "I was here. Did you notice? Did I make any impact at all on this world?" Because of this desire for significance, I believe it's in all our hearts to declare . . .

Because I breathe, someone else can breathe a little easier
Because I walk, I can take someone by the hand and help them walk
Because I see, I can see the pain of someone else and provide a balm

Because I talk, I can speak for the one who can't form the words
Because I sing, I can place a melody in someone's heart
Because I touch, I can place my fingerprint in the soul of another
Because I have, I can give
Because I'm here, I can do something there
Because I hear, I can listen
Because I know, I can solve
Because of my strength, I can help overcome a weakness
Because I understand, I can bring a new understanding
Because I learn, I can teach
Because I take up space, I can fill an emptiness, a void in someone's life
Because I love, you are loved

I was here.

A Ceremony of Significance

Can you tell how powerful this idea of significance is? It's so powerful that even at that final moment when someone's voice in this earth is finally and forever silenced what do we do? We gather around to acknowledge that they were here in a ceremony we call a funeral or memorial service.

I've probably preached over 2,000 funerals in my many years of ministry. I can't explain it, but I suppose that's one of the gifts God has given me, the ability to minister to people in that dark time of grieving. Of course, every pastor preaches his or her share of funerals. Many feel awkward or at a loss and merely endure, doing the best they can. But I feel an anointing from the Lord each and every time I preach a funeral. When I step up to minister to the grieving, I feel like I'm stepping into my destiny.

Over the years I've gotten to know quite a few funeral directors. I always talk to them and encourage them to call me if they ever encounter a family who has no pastor. I've recognized that I have this unique calling to go into a family of people I've never met and somehow learn just a few important things about the person who has died. Then at the funeral, I'm able to share not only Jesus but a little bit about the life of their precious loved one, their daddy or mother.

I've sat with grieving family members thousands of times and held them as they wept. I've seen them gather around the casket and pat the cold marble face and hold on to the lapels of their loved one, not wanting to let them go. "Oh, that was my sweet momma. Let me tell you about her," they'll say. "Let me tell you who she was. Her personality, her infectious smile, and her kind eyes," or "My daddy had the strongest hands. They felt soft at times whenever I needed comfort, but boy, they sure could lay down the law too." You really can't imagine the things they tell me in those intimate times. You can hear the words wash over you and feel their warmth wrap around you.

I was here.

A Father's Significance

My daddy died when I was only thirteen years old. My mother didn't pass until many years later, and I was privileged to be able to preach at her funeral. I focused on the celebration of life and told stories about the tremendous significance she had in our family.

I'm the youngest of seven children, a "late in life" child. I used to tell my parents that I was one of those unplanned, best mistakes they ever made. When my mom was forty-four years old, she'd gone to see the doctor about having a hysterectomy. After an initial examination, the doctor came out into the waiting room and told my father, "We can't do the hysterectomy." My dad was surprised and said, "What's the problem?" The doctor replied, "Well . . . there's a baby! We can't do the procedure!" My dad couldn't believe it. He was fifty-six years old when I was born.

My dad never ran for office, never made a lot of money or influenced a lot of people in an outward kind of way. He was a World War II vet and worked for the Detroit, Toledo, and Ironton railroad for thirty years. He raised seven kids in a little wood frame house nestled in the hills and never really went anywhere except for when he was in the war.

But this man, who never accomplished much by the world's standards, made me into the man I am today. And influenced me in a thousand different ways, some I'm still discovering today. The people who encounter me, those who have heard me preach, or who are members of the church I pastor, even those of you who are reading this book are influenced indirectly by my father. He's found true significance, even years after death, because of his impact on me and my brothers and sisters.

A Legacy of Significance

I was lamenting one day over the fact that my children never had the chance to meet my dad. Fortunately, all four of my children were privileged to know my mother. But none of my kids got a chance to meet and get to know their granddad. When I was growing up, my dad was a hard man. He didn't come to know Christ until about six years before he died. He spent most of his life as an agnostic.

But I remember Dad would do this thing where he'd clap his hands when he'd had his say in a matter. He would let me debate with him, and we'd argue back and forth. I'd be pushing my opinion, trying to convince him of my point of view, when suddenly he'd clap his hands and say, "I've had my say." Now when that happened, you'd better stop the argument right there. We all learned as kids that when he clapped his hands and said he was done, that's exactly what he meant; the debate was over and done with.

So, I was lamenting the fact that my kids had never had the chance to get to know my father when Katie started to banter back and forth with me about something she wanted. She couldn't have been but five or six years old at the time, but she was arguing with me, trying to get her way. And before I even realized what I was doing, I clapped my hands together. I didn't even think about it. It was just a natural reaction. I clapped my hands and said, "I've had my say."

It wasn't until the words had escaped my mouth that I realized the significance of what had just happened. Katie had never met my dad. But in that fleeting moment, she got just a little taste of who he was. That's because there's a residual of my dad still alive within me.

No doubt we've all experienced moments just like this. We do something or say something and think, "Wow, that's just like my mom or dad." We look in the mirror and catch glimpses of people who lived long ago. We say things, things we learned from our parents or older relatives, bosses, teachers or coaches, folks who have gone on before us that continue to affect and influence the lives of people in our own sphere.

If you think back, you are who you are because of the significance of someone in your life who passed their significance on to you. The truth is, we are all sitting in the shade of trees we didn't plant. And this significance stretches out to the horizon of the future as well. The importance of who we are will last for generations in the lives of those we touch when we're no longer on this earth.

I was here.

Those words, those three short words, just eight little letters, reveal the deep-down human desire for significance. It's there in the beginning, in the baby's cry and it's there at the very end, as death rattles in our throat. We want to leave our mark on this earth. We want to shout it from the rooftops and carve it in a tree in the woods. We want everyone to know . . . I was here.

2

The Power of Anonymity

Who Was That Masked Man?

As kids growing up, we always looked forward to watching our shows on television every Saturday morning. When I was a kid, we only had three channels, and they were all pretty fuzzy, the signal being just strong enough to barely make out what was going on.

My brother Tim would always try to get a better picture by going outside and twisting the pole that the television antenna was mounted to. He'd be outside twisting, and we'd be inside shouting, "Just a little more . . . THERE! Stop right there! Nope, now go back the other way! STOP! There, that's good." Of course, the second he let go of the pole; the reception would go back to being fuzzy again.

So, through snowy reception, we'd watch shows like Schoolhouse Rock, Bugs Bunny, Daffy Duck, The Road Runner, Yosemite Sam, and many of the other classic cartoons from days gone by. And then invariably in the afternoon, there would always be an episode of The Lone Ranger.

Most episodes were all pretty similar. The Lone Ranger and Tonto would come riding into town in a cloud of dust, the Lone Ranger riding his white steed "Silver" and Tonto riding his paint horse "Scout." The town would usually be in turmoil over some situation caused by the bad guys. The two heroes would save the day, and they'd ride off into the sunset after Silver would rear up on his hind legs and the Lone Ranger would shout, "HI

HO SILVER. AWAY!" As they disappeared into the distant high country chaparral one of the town's people would turn to another and say, "Who was that masked man?" Although he'd saved the town, he chose to wear a mask and stay anonymous. No one knew his name.

You Don't Need to Know My Name

Our true significance isn't about recognition or acclaim. It's rooted in our relationship with God and in connecting to the core of the person He made us to be when He reached into our mother's womb and knit us together.

Significance is not found in fanfare or name recognition. Some of the most significant people in the Bible are never mentioned by name. Our story from 2 Kings about the man who lost the ax head in the river is never named, and yet we're being influenced by his experience all these thousands of years later. We're being challenged by a man whose name we'll never know.

I remember early in my ministry, I was just a twenty-three-year-old preacher, pastoring a church. Admittedly, I was probably too young for so much responsibility, but the Lord blessed, and the church grew. It had grown so much that folks no longer knew where to park.

I didn't know what else to do but go out before the service started and shake some hands and help direct people to another lot around back where they could park. I remember one Sunday morning a family pulled in who had just visited for the first time the previous Sunday. They were driving the family truck and the man, whose name was Randy, got out and said, "What are you doing, Pastor?"

I said, "I'm directing traffic and parking cars." He said, "What are you doing that for?" "Well," I said, "nobody knew where to park, and we have this space around back for overflow, so I'm directing them back there." In a moment of inspiration, I continued, "Randy, why don't you and your sons help me with that next Sunday. You guys come out here before the service and help park cars." Randy smiled at me and said, "Sure, we'll do that for you!"

Over the years Randy became a great friend. Eventually, he became one of the elders of the church and even began to travel with me when I preached revivals and camps and conferences around the country. He'd go along with me and help carry bags, set things up, and handle a myriad of other details allowing me to focus on the preaching.

We'd fly in or drive into some big camp meeting or conference, and he'd be right there by my side in case I needed anything, anything at all. He was always a faithful servant. It wasn't odd for folks to come up to me to engage in conversation, then turn to Randy and ask, "Now, who are you?" Randy would always say, "You don't need to know my name." He always made that statement, "You don't need to know my name. I'm just here to serve."

A Tract Left in the Door

Harry S Truman is often quoted as saying, "It is amazing what you can accomplish if you do not care who gets the credit." Many years later, Ronald Reagan had the quote on a plaque mounted on the wall in the Oval Office.

That adage is true in the Kingdom as well. God can do a lot through anonymity. When we can get our egos out of the way and make a way for God and His glory to come into the situation, anything can happen.

I've often asked the question, "Would you give your life to save the world if no one knew your name?" If our significance and worth came with the cost of anonymity, would it be worth the price?

Our significance isn't found in what we may do to gain attention in this world. As a result, many times our value can go unnoticed, not recognized by the world. But it's not about doing things to be noticed or doing things to gain attention. It's about being the person God created us to be even if it means we must remain anonymous.

Part of who I am today, a pastor and a preacher, I am because of my Sunday school teacher. For over forty years, Harry Thacker taught Sunday school to scores of little boys in the same small church classroom. Like layers and layers of stone and concrete, this man helped establish and strengthen our spiritual foundations, teaching us stories from the Bible about Jesus and other people of significance.

The world may never know Harry Thacker's name. But over his decades of teaching, he influenced not only me but my brothers and dozens of others who in turn have affected hundreds, even thousands more . . . all because of the life of Harry Thacker. Except for the brief mention in this book, you may have never read about him. He was no celebrity, no one special by the world's standard, but he was exactly who God created him to be.

What about the significance of the unnamed person who left Wellston, Ohio, one day and drove up the hill on that county road? At the top of the hill, he had to slow the car to only twenty miles per hour to make the big curve in the street. About a mile past that curve to the left, backed up against the trees and the railroad track was the home that my mom and dad lived in at the time. The place still sits there on that gravel road to this day, and the railroad track still runs through the backyard.

The unnamed person took a drive on that gravel road outside of Wellston and put a Gospel tract on the front door of that house by the railroad track. He didn't just drive on by. He stopped the car and made an effort to get out and put a tract in the door, just hoping someone would find it and read it and may be changed by it.

At the time, my mom was a twenty-seven-year-old heathen who would have nothing to do with God. My dad was a World War II veteran who, when he enlisted, had to claim he was a "Christian" because you had to claim a religion. When they asked him what religion he was, he said, "I don't claim nothing." The man asked him, "You don't believe in God?" Dad could only say, "I'm not sure." My dad was basically an agnostic, but that wasn't an option, so they called him a "Christian" and gave him a Catholic Bible.

Little did that man who left the tract know that his efforts would change the course of a family's history. My mom had just returned home from getting groceries that day while my dad was still at work. She opened the front door to go inside and noticed the tract as it fell to the floor. She picked it up and read it. Of course, this was many years before I was born, but I've heard the story many times. Something in that tract grabbed her heart and would not let go. We know today that "something" was the Holy Spirit and He was convicting her heart.

She didn't know why but over the next few days she was miserable and couldn't sleep. It was as if the weight of the world had settled like a heavy wet blanket upon her shoulders. In the evenings she'd fix supper and pull up to the table and fix her plate, but she couldn't eat. She went to her mother and said, "Mom, I don't know what's wrong with me." My grandmother told her, "I didn't raise you in church. But I can tell you what's wrong. The Lord is calling you. You need to go to that church in town and pray to Him. I think they have services on Wednesday nights. Just go and they'll pray with you."

So, when Wednesday rolled around, she went out and tried to start the car to make the drive to town. But the car didn't start. So, she went over to dad's work car, but it didn't start either. The strange thing was that both those cars were in perfect working order and had no trouble starting the next day. But that evening they were dead, so she had to walk the three and a half miles into town.

To listen to her tell the story, "On that walk to church it felt like the weight of the world was on my shoulders and cinder blocks were attached to my feet. Every step was a struggle. My legs felt as heavy as iron. But I couldn't wait to get to the church. I had no idea what to expect when I got there. I just knew I couldn't keep living the way I felt."

She walked into the church, and after listening to the sermon, she went down front and knelt at the altar. The folks there at the church told her what to say, and she started praying. She said that all at once the wet blanket that sat so heavily upon her shoulders was lifted and it felt like a jackhammer busted up the bricks from around her feet. She said, "It was so light walking home. The sky had never looked so pretty, and my heart had never felt so good. I had never felt so clean in all my life." From that moment on, she served God for the rest of her life raising all seven of her kids in the church.

The significance of that story is this. I've traveled and preached all over the world. And almost all of our family, kids, and grandkids serve God in some capacity or another. It was all due to a simple tract left in the door of a little house at the end of a country road. Somebody did something that they might've felt was of little significance at the time, with no fanfare, no accolade, no pat on the back or acclaim. They probably didn't get special recognition on Sunday morning for leaving the tract, and they didn't get a card in the mail from the pastor. Nothing.

No one has any idea who put the tract on Mom's door that would change the course of our lives forever. Not to mention the hundreds and thousands of people who have been influenced by my ministry over the last thirty years. I have no idea who that someone is to this day, but let me assure you, Heaven knows their name. Heaven knows who they are. Eternity bears the mark.

The Great Unnamed

There's the daddy who works hard to fight for his family, to put bread on the table and provide a warm place to sleep on cold nights. There's the mother who loves unconditionally with very little in return. Or the pastor who is faithful to his calling and leads a few souls who are in his charge to hear and follow the will of God. There's the activist who puts his life on the line for the cause, the teacher who works tirelessly to make a difference in someone's life . . . all without so much as an apple on her desk. No one knows their names, but they've brought significance to their world.

There once was a Scottish preacher at a little church way out in the country. His elders approached him one day after he'd been preaching at the church for about a year and said to him, "Pastor, don't you think you should call it quits? You've only had one convert this whole year." The pastor nodded his head and said, "You're probably right, it has been a difficult year.

My only convert was the wee lad, Bobby Moffat and he's so young we probably shouldn't even count him."

But the old preacher stuck with it, and a few years later, young Bobby came to the pastor and said, "Pastor, do you think that I could ever learn to preach? I feel something in my heart telling me that's what I'm supposed to do. If I could lead lost souls to Christ, that would make my heart happy." The pastor answered, "Well, I think you should at least give it a try!"

And try he did. Throughout his long career, Robert Moffat grew to be a great theologian and a translator of the Bible. He established a mighty mission work in Africa, and when he returned to England many years later, the King of England and the British Parliament rose from their seats to greet him as a mark of respect.

But what about that humble old country preacher who led wee Bobby in the Sinner's Prayer? What about that man who almost turned his back on his calling and quit his pastorate because of his discouragement over just one convert after a whole year of ministry? He's anonymous, and he's lost to history. Nobody knows his name.

What about the Sunday school teacher who kept pestering a simple shoe salesperson until he finally accepted Jesus. The salesman's name was Dwight L. Moody, who later became a powerful evangelist and founder of the Moody Bible Institute. But almost no one remembers Edward Kimball, his Sunday school teacher. Or what about the Sunday school teacher who taught Billy Graham as a boy and led him to Jesus. We know who Billy Graham is, but the teacher's name has faded into the past.

I could go on and on. Sure there are those down through history who have made it all about themselves, going for the acclaim and the adoration of the crowd. They yearned for the attention, the position or title, or the microphone or camera. They cry, "That's my song" or "my seat." "That's my parking place," "my high-rise apartment" or "my mansion." "Look at all I was able to accomplish!"

But it wasn't about that for the unnamed. They were able to find significance in deeper things, in eternal ways. I love to read Hebrews chapter 11, the Bible's "Hall of Faith." There are a few names listed in that chapter, people we've loved to study through the years, people who are certainly admirable and significant in their own right. But my favorite passage of that whole chapter comes near the end after the list of named people of faith,

"And others had trial of cruel mockings and scourgings, yea, moreover of bonds and imprisonment: They were stoned, they were sawn asunder, were tempted, were slain with the sword: they wandered about in sheepskins and goatskins; being destitute, afflicted, tormented; (Of whom the world was not worthy:) . . . " (Hebrews 11:36-38).

I love that last phrase, "Of whom the world was not worthy." In other words, these people, these unnamed saints who have gone before us, the world is not worthy of them. People will never know their names.

You're Not Home Yet

I love the story of the missionary and his wife returning home from Africa. After decades on the mission field, they were worn out and weary. Their health was in decline, and they were ready to retire. While buying their tickets, they learned that they just happened to be booked on the same ship to America as the former president of the United States, Theodore Roosevelt, who had been in Africa hunting for big game.

The hoopla began on the ship during the journey. Exuberant fanfare and adoration seemed to follow in the wake of the great man while the missionary and his wife could walk the ship's decks in anonymity even though they'd spent their entire adult lives in Africa building schools, churches, and hospitals and preaching the Gospel from one end of the continent to the other. None of that seemed to matter. They weren't recognized at all . . . in any way. No one knew who they were.

If it was bad during the journey, things got even worse when they pulled into New York harbor. There were bands on hand to play, streamers flying through the air, and even a few dignitaries had shown up to make speeches.

The way it often does, the old missionary's flesh began to complain. He said to his wife, "I just don't get it. We've given our whole life to helping the people of Africa. We've built schools and hospitals, and we've preached the Gospel to thousands. And this guy, he goes and shoots a lion or an elephant, and everyone gathers around to praise him. There's no one here to even say a simple 'thank you for all you've done' to us."

Of course, the missionary's wife speaks to him in the way only a wife can get away with, "Honey, I think you've got the wrong attitude about this. Maybe you need to go to the Lord and ask Him about it."

So after they got off the ship and settled in their simple little flat, he shut himself in the bedroom and began to pray. "Lord, I don't understand. We've given our lives to help people, and during our journey home, no one recognized us at all. And when we got to the docks, there was no one there to greet us, no bands playing for all we've done, no appreciation, no articles in the paper. Nothing. But this guy, he comes home from hunting animals and gets the royal welcome!"

The Lord interrupted the missionary's prayer and simply said, "But son, you're not home yet."

Our significance and worth go beyond the bounds of this earth and time and humanity itself. Our significance transcends this finite existence and extends to eternity.

You, dear reader, are of great worth. Your significance is found in Him, not in the accolades or fanfare or position or title. Your relevance has nothing to do with how many friends you have on Facebook or Instagram. Your significance is wrapped up in your identity, which is who God made you to be. The discovery of who you are is what's going to leave the mark in this earth even though the world may never know your name.

3

Living with a
False Identity

What's In a Name?

Mark Twain once said, "The two most important days of your life are the day you are born, and the day you find out why." Most of us can probably figure out the first important day, the day of our birth, but sadly, very few of us ever experience the second. In fact, I would say that the epic struggle of humanity is the search for why we were born.

At some point in our lives, every one of us is going to ask the question of why we were born, what's it all about? Who are we? What's our identity? And it's critical that we learn the answer because identity becomes the framework that we build our lives around. Our identity is the filter through which we experience the world around us. We see, hear, understand, and process the world through the lens of how we see ourselves. If we are insecure about the basics of who we are, then we're much more likely to be swayed by others' views and their own opinion of who we are.

From the time we are born, we're assaulted by the world trying to press us into its mold. Many of us have been blessed to have loving parents, skilled mentors, teachers, and coaches in our lives. But no one is perfect. Even loving parents can try to shape you into their version of who you should be instead of nurturing the person God created you to be.

The truth is, our identity comes from the father, not only our earthly father but our Heavenly Father as well. We carry our father's DNA; we carry his character and maybe even his appearance. But from the time we are born, we face a constant struggle from our enemy, the devil, to try to shape us into something we are not.

Let me introduce a bit of truth here for you. John 1:12 says, "But as many as received him, to them gave he power to become the sons of God, even to them that believe on his name."

You know what that means? It merely means that if you've received Jesus as your Lord and Savior and put your faith and trust in Him alone, it doesn't matter what anyone else says or what anyone else does, YOU ARE HIS CHILD! This is so important to know because from the moment we are born the enemy will come to challenge your identity, your place in Christ. He will even change your identity if he can.

It's sad but true, because of the fall of Adam, this world is cursed, and its nature is a cursed nature, so eventually, everybody will feed into a lie about you. Something will happen, circumstances, disappointments, traumas, and tragedies will occur in your life, and they will twist you and bend you and begin to shape you into someone you are not. It happens subtly, and you don't even realize your thinking is being reshaped. Soon you'll be convinced that you were born that way when the truth is that the world and the enemy have been molding and shaping you since the day you were born.

The life-altering incident doesn't even have to be something big and terrible. Sure, many times it's death or divorce or disease or some other major event that rocks your world. But it can be something small and seemingly insignificant. I've been shocked to hear of people who have built their whole lives on a false identity that they've adopted because of something that happened in their lives that seemed trivial at the time. Friend, the truth is, there's nothing trivial when it comes to your identity.

Captured and Renamed

In the book of Daniel chapter 3, King Nebuchadnezzar took Israel captive and brought Israel's best and brightest young people back to Babylon. But he couldn't have these young men growing up with their previous beliefs and traditions. He needed to begin the indoctrination process right away. He had to change them. So he changed the clothes they wore and the food they ate and taught them a new language to speak. But the king knew that to truly change their identities he was going to have to change their names.

You've probably heard these names before, Shadrach, Meshach, and Abednego. But did you realize that those are not the names those boys were given at birth? Those were their Babylonian names given them by King Nebuchadnezzar. Their Hebrew names had much different meanings.

Shadrach's real name, the name given him by his parents and by God was Hananiah, which means, "the Lord is gracious." But Nebuchadnezzar couldn't tolerate that. So he changed Hananiah's name to Shadrach, which means, "I am fearful of God." Can you see how powerful and how damaging that name change could have been? By changing his name, Nebuchadnezzar was attempting to change the core of who Shadrach was.

What about Meshach? Meshach means, "I am of little value or of no account." Can you imagine the damaging effect of being called that name every time someone tried to get your attention? Especially when you consider that his real name, Mishael, means, "Who is like God." King Nebuchadnezzar flipped his name around and gave him a name with the exact opposite meaning to the name he was given at birth.

Mishael's name was a compelling description of his destiny, "Who is like God," or "Made in His image." The Word of God over his life was, "You will be like Me." But the king comes along and says to him, "You're living a lie, you're nothing but a little liar, and you'll never amount to anything." And he changes his name to Meschach, which means, "I am of little value or no account."

Does this sound familiar to you? Have you had people in your life, even people you trust and look up to, try to define who you are, calling you by a different name? "You'll never amount to anything, and you're worthless." Teachers who tell you you're not smart enough, coaches telling you that you'll never make the team, or even parents who tell you that you're not worth loving. All these statements effectively do the job of "renaming" us. And we live our lives believing the lie instead of the truth. We live out our lives believing that we will never achieve significance just because we've allowed others to rename us.

The problem is that we'll never fully reach our significance when we allow other people to remake us into their image of who we are instead of living our life as the person God made us to be.

Now let's not forget about Abednego. His real name was Azariah, which means, "The Lord has helped me." But the name Abednego means, "Servant of Nebo." It's as if Nebuchadnezzar was saying, "I'm not going to let you look to your God to save you. I'll give you another god to serve and to worship. You'll have to look to this other god for the things in life you need like money, shelter . . . and significance."

In all three cases, Nebuchadnezzar was doing much more than just changing the name on their name tags or giving them a Babylonian name instead of their given Hebrew name. No, it was much more sinister, and powerful, than that. He was trying to change who they were and how they thought of themselves. He wanted to change their identities.

The king couldn't permit these Hebrew slaves to believe that the Lord is gracious or that they were made in God's image or that the Lord would always be there to help them. He had to try to change their identities and he started that process by changing their names. The world attempts to do the same thing with us.

Nebuchadnezzar called these young men something different in order to change them. But when God created them, He knit worth and significance into their very cellular structure. The same is true of us. Our worth was placed in us at conception, but from the time we are born, Satan, sin, fallen man, our worldly culture, all try to change our names and call us something we're not.

This Is Not Me

This is why there are so many in our world today who suffer from an identity crisis. They do not know who they are born to be. And the cry of their hearts is the same as the man hiking in the woods, "I am here! Look at me! This is who I am!" When all the while, the world is trying to push us into its mold saying, "No, you're not that. You're something else entirely."

That's the struggle, the tension we all live with. We believe ourselves to be one thing while the world and others try to push us into being something else.

I remember some years ago, a woman showed up at church one Sunday morning for the very first time. She and the others with her came right down the aisle and sat on the second row. It was a strange situation. She had the man she was married to sitting on one side of her and her current boyfriend sitting on the other side! Talk about dysfunctional relationships!

I saw these folks come in and I knew who they were. I got up to preach and preached Christ, His grace and His justice. The Holy Spirit fell on her and convicted her, and when I gave the altar call, she stepped out into the aisle and came down front. She was prayed for and was born again.

We learned that because of all the chaos and dysfunction in her life that she hadn't spoken to her children in many years. That very day she reached out to her oldest son and said, "If you have any interest in seeing me, then come to the church at this address tonight at 6:00."

Well, God was in it (He's always in the process of restoring relationships!) and her son showed up and brought with him his half brother. That night the Holy Spirit touched those boys' hearts, and they both stepped out into the aisle and came forward for the altar call to accept Christ.

So, the two boys started attending church faithfully with their mother. Now the half brother's father was not too keen on them going to church. He was the ex-husband of the woman, and he hated her. He'd kept away from her and hadn't seen her in over twenty-five years. The man had been raised Catholic his whole life but never really practiced. He hadn't been to church since he left home over forty years before. So, he came to church one Sunday just to see what was going on.

After the message he was convicted by the Holy Spirit and, just like the others, he stepped out and came down to the altar and got saved! Afterward, he came up to me and told me, "I came to this church to find out what my crazy ex-wife has gotten my kids involved in. I wanted to know if this was a cult or not and I wanted to see what kind of guy you were. I was going to try and figure out what was going on. I was fully prepared to step in and rescue them! But I'll be damned if you didn't get me too!" Yep, he really did say that. Of course, he'd just been saved, and his language hadn't been renewed yet!

So, he started coming to church regularly too. There was the man, his current wife, his two sons and daughter and her husband. All in addition to his ex-wife, her husband and her boyfriend. By now this crazy family took up a full two rows in the church! And God continued to work in all their lives.

One Sunday morning his ex-wife was praying up at the front of the church, and the man went up to her and hugged her and said, "I forgive you." Then he asked her, "Will you come to eat dinner at my house sometime?" And she said she would.

That week the man called me and said, "I need you to come over to my house and see me." So, I told him I'd come over. When I got to his house he said, "What have you done to me?" I was surprised and confused at the question and asked, "What are you talking about? I haven't done anything to you." He said, "This is not me! I'm acting in ways that are completely out of character. This is not me."

He took a deep breath and continued, "Did you see me last Sunday? I went up and hugged and forgave someone I've hated for over twenty-five years. I even invited her to my house for dinner! What in the world is that about?" He said, "You've got to stop whatever you're doing to me. I can't figure out who I am anymore. This is not me."

I smiled because I knew that the Holy Spirit must've been at work in him. You see, even while the world is trying to change you, God is always at your side, shaping you into His image. He desires to reveal to you the identity that He placed within you before you were even born.

Once the man gave his life to Jesus, God began the work of changing his identity. No longer would he be known by names like "Unforgiveness, Bitterness, or Hate. God was changing his name to "Forgiveness, Patience, and Love," molding him into a brand-new creature.

I looked at the man and said, "Could it be that for the last fifty-five years you've been acting out of character and now God is transforming you, giving you a whole new identity? Maybe you're just now starting to step into your real character, the person you truly are." He dropped his head and smiled. He said, "Maybe you're right, Pastor, maybe you're right."

God is in the business of transforming us. He wants to take us and change us from someone motivated and driven by sin and selfish impulses and make us into a whole new creature. He wants to give us a new name and a fresh new identity.

4

The Difficult Place of Transition

Wrestling with a New Identity

So, what does it look like when God begins to work in you to reveal to you your true identity? Just like King Nebuchadnezzar, God often starts by changing your name. There's a relationship between your identity and your name. The enemy knows this . . . but God is well aware of it too. God is the One who designed us that way.

Think about it, how many times in the Scriptures do you see that when God chose to work on somebody, He'd change their name? As you leaf through the Old Testament, you'll find that Abram, which means "high father" was changed to Abraham, meaning "father of a multitude." And his wife, Sarai, which means, "my princess" was changed to Sarah, which means "mother of nations" (Genesis 17). And I love the story of God changing Jacob's name to Israel.

Here was Jacob, whose desire for significance and identity was so strong that even at birth, on his way out of the womb, he took hold of his brother's ankle, literally grasping at anything he could to become the firstborn. Even as a newborn, he was desperate to be known, he desired significance. It was as if his very first cry uttered the words, "I am here! Don't overlook me!"

From that moment forward, Jacob's life was a constant yearning and striving for significance. Of course, most of the time, he went about it the wrong way. He lied and cheated, stole and swindled. He thought he might finally achieve significance by stealing his big brother Esau's blessing from his father, Isaac. Jacob succeeded in getting the blessing, but he wasn't able to grasp the significance he so desperately desired.

Jacob never fully understood his significance until the night he wrestled with God, crying out, "I will not let you go until you give me your blessing!" (see Genesis 32:26). He knew the blessing he received from his earthly father wasn't enough. He had to have what only the Heavenly Father could give him, and he was determined not to let go until he got it.

So, God says to him, "No longer will you be Jacob," which means "to follow, or to be behind." "From now on you'll be known as Israel" (v. 28), which means, "One who has been strong against God." To mark the moment, God touched Jacob's hip and caused him to walk with a limp for the rest of his life. Jacob, the follower, could never realize his significance as a strong leader until he became Israel and understood the person God made him to be.

It was as if God said to Jacob (now Israel), "I want to change you. I want to change you from the person you were into a whole new person." So, God's first step in Jacob's transformation process was to change his name to Israel.

And isn't it interesting . . . his name today marks a little, out-of-the-way strip of land on the eastern shore of the Mediterranean Sea. It's less than 300 miles long from top to bottom and only 85 miles wide at its widest point. And yet, it's often at the epicenter of world events. We hear about what's going on in that little country almost every night as we watch the news.

Your name represents so much more than just what people call you. When God renames you, that new name represents something more, something significant about who you are, your role here on earth, your identity, and your destiny.

It's like when you were little and your parents bought you shoes that were way too big knowing that you'd eventually grow into them. God purposely gives you an identity, a name that is too big for you. It's way more than you'd ever be able to live up to or accomplish on your own. But He knows that the more you hold fast to Him, the more you will be like Him, and the more you are like Him, the more you'll be able to walk in your new identity.

Simon Becomes Peter

So it was with Simon. His brother brought him to Jesus. And as soon as Christ saw him, He told Simon, "I know who you are. I know exactly who you are. You are Simon, son of Jonas. But I'm going to call you Peter. Oh, I know who you are. Your daddy called you Simon and your momma called you Simon. The kids and the teachers you grew up with at school all called you Simon. The men down at the docks called you Simon. I get it. You've been called Simon for as long as you can remember.

"But I want you to know that the moment I laid eyes on you I saw something else in you. I saw a purpose much greater than catching fish in the sea. I saw a role for you to play that was so much bigger. I know you have always seen yourself the same way others see you . . . as Simon. But I have a new identity for you. I see you as Peter" (John 1:42).

I appreciate the fact that whenever we come in contact with the Savior, He never leaves us as He found us. He is always faithful to change us, making us into a brand-new creature. But this transition between who we were and who God is making us to be is rarely smooth. It's a struggle. Jacob wrestled with God, and we often fight with Him too as we go through this transformative process. You've heard of "growing pains"? We all experience these pains as we let go of who the world has shaped us to be and grab onto who God has created us to be.

Simon didn't immediately become a different person. He struggled and went back and forth between living like Simon and living like Peter as he "tried on" the new name, the new person Jesus was calling him to be.

Peter's Rough Day

I love the story from Matthew 16 where Jesus asked the disciples, "Who do people say that I am?" The disciples immediately chimed in with a chorus of answers, "Some say that you are John the Baptist, some say the prophet Elijah or Jeremiah."

But Jesus wanted to put a finer point on things. He looked at them and said, "But who do YOU say I am?" Peter immediately said, "You are the Christ, the Son of the living God."

Jesus looked at him and told him, "You're right! And let Me tell you something else. Your momma and daddy didn't teach you that. You didn't learn it in school or at the synagogue. God Himself revealed it to you. And let Me remind you, you are Peter, which means 'rock' and upon this rock I will build My church!" (Matthew 16:13-19).

But look . . . just a few verses later Jesus is talking about how He now must go to Jerusalem to be killed. Peter again is first to speak up and says, "No! Jesus, we will never let that happen to You!" But Jesus looks at Peter and rebukes him saying, "Get behind Me, Satan!"

That's quite a transition! Earlier, Peter had had a pure revelation, straight from God about who Jesus is. I mean to tell you he went to church that morning and he heard God's voice clearly. He shouted and he ran the aisle. He went forward and fell out in the Holy Ghost! Peter had heard from God!

And now, just a few verses later, Jesus is calling him Satan and telling him to get behind Him! Now that's a rough day. When you go from hearing straight from God to being called Satan by Jesus . . . that's a bad day for sure!

But is that not a picture of us? We find ourselves in a groove. We're walking right by Jesus's side. He's so close we can hear even His whispers as we walk in the lush garden in the cool of the day. And just a minute later we're wandering in the barren wilderness with evil on our minds. Just like that, we go from being Simon to Peter and then back to Simon again. This is the struggle, the wrestling match I'm talking about.

We transition between the person I've been and the new person He says I am. We go back and forth between the two. We tell ourselves, "This is how I feel. But this is what God says about me."

Jesus Prays for Us

You see, Simon is in transition, which is good news for all of us. Because if the Lord was that patient with Simon, He'll be that patient with you and with me. In Luke 22:31 Jesus says, "Simon, Simon," (by the way, you know it's not going to be good when Jesus has to say your name twice!) He says, "Satan hath desired to have you, that he may sift you as wheat:"

But look what Jesus says next, "But I have prayed for thee, that thy faith fail not . . . " (Luke 22:32). Why is Jesus praying for Peter? Because He knows that Peter is going to mess up. He's going to deny ever knowing Jesus. And yet Jesus prays for him anyway. Notice that He doesn't pray that Peter won't MESS up. He prays that Peter won't GIVE up.

We will all mess up at some point in the search for significance and identity. We'll have days where we feel like we're walking in the sunshine, receiving a constant stream of divine revelation, only to find ourselves, a day later, walking through the valley of the shadow of death.

We all have to make several attempts at the new identity before it takes. We'll go back and forth wrestling and struggling with who we were meant to be. And the shame of it is that often it seems that the church has a very low tolerance for this process of messy transitions. There's an attitude that we have to have it all figured out before we even step through the church doors. It's no wonder the lost have such a hard time coming to church. In many ways . . . they're not welcome. I'm not so sure Peter himself would be welcomed into many modern-day churches.

And yet, Jesus looks beyond our mess ups and prays that we won't give up! He knows we're going to get it wrong. He knows we're going to fall short. He wants us to keep on going. He knows that we will fail, but no failure will make our significance null and void. Our mess ups will never take God's purpose out of our reach. That's what the redemption of the cross is all about. Because of the cross of Christ, our destiny is always within reach.

It's like our story of the man who lost the ax head in the river. God not only caused the ax head to float, but He also made it within reach, so the man could retrieve it. If you don't give up, God will not only reveal your identity and purpose to you, He'll bring it within reach, so you can grasp it and find true significance.

So, what's the key to keep going? What's the key to not giving up, the key to success? Just this . . . you have to let go of Simon before you can become Peter. You have to let go of what the world has made you before you can embrace the person God has created you to be. You have to let go of that old identity before you can fully follow Christ and before God can truly transform you and give you a new name.

Follow Me

I want to close this chapter by telling you one more story about Peter. In John 21, Peter had denied Christ; he'd failed and fallen short. Jesus had been crucified and the world of the disciples had been upended. Peter was feeling his failure deeply and told his fellow disciples that he was going fishing. In essence, he was saying, "I'm giving up on being Peter. I've made a complete mess of things, and I'm done. I'm going back to my old life as Simon."

So, Peter goes out with the other disciples to fish. And while he's fishing, he sees Jesus on the beach and immediately jumps in and swims ashore to be with Jesus. The other disciples follow in the boat, and they meet up with Peter and Jesus.

During a lull in their conversation, Jesus looks at Peter and says, "Simon, do you love Me?" And Peter responds, "You know I do, Lord." Jesus asks him the same thing again . . . two more times. Confused, Peter says again, "Yes, Lord. You know I love You." Jesus responds, "Feed My lambs."

Then He reveals to Peter, "Simon, you are going to die the same way I died . . . on a cross." In the transition, Jesus will lead us to this point of surrender. He will put all His cards on the table and say, "This is where we are going. Are you willing to give up what you've been, what the world has said you are, what the enemy has tried to change you into? Will you let go of the old you and follow Me into your new identity? Will you let go of Simon, so you can become Peter?"

At some point you have to come to this place, this impasse, where you lay your all on the altar of sacrifice, surrendering yourself to the absolute lordship of Jesus Christ. Being willing to give your life entirely and completely to Him until you get to the place where you can honestly say, "Take Simon but give me Peter. Take this whole world but give me Jesus. I won't turn back, I won't turn back," you'll never experience your true identity. You'll never find the significance you so desperately desire.

My friend, don't turn back! Don't give up! Make the decision that you will not go back to the person you were. Commit to walking forward and not stepping backward. Set your face like a flint to follow Jesus in every way, always. Declare the words of that old hymn, "Though none go with me, still I will follow!"

5

Hey, Pick Me! The Willingness to Be Chosen No Matter What

When I was a kid, probably 5th or 6th grade, something like that, I remember being released from school for recess right after lunch. At Central School, where I attended, the playground was around on the side of the building. It was also on that side of the building where the school's air-conditioning units were. They were surrounded by a chain link fence to protect them. It was in that part of the playground where we played a big game of kickball every day.

This was something all the boys in school wanted to be a part of. A couple of the more athletic boys would be captains in charge of choosing teams. The rest of us would all line up in a straight line with just one thought on our minds, "Hey, pick me!"

We'd jump up and down, waving our hands, yelling out, "Hey, pick me! Pick me!" There was just something deep down in all of us that so desperately wanted to be chosen to be on the team, to get to play kickball.

In our game, if you wanted to kick a home run, you couldn't just kick the ball as far as you could because once the ball went out in the street a few times, the teacher wouldn't give it back. So, the challenge was to kick the ball into that fenced-in area where the air conditioners were . . . that was our home run. Every kid wanted the chance to step up to the plate and kick that ball all the way to the air conditioners. HOME RUN!

I remember feeling that way nearly every school day during those years. I wanted to be picked. I wanted to be on the team. I wanted my chance to try to kick a home run into the fence.

The Cry of the Heart of Mankind

I think there's something inside the heart of all humans that cries out, "Hey, pick me!" I'm sure you've seen it in your kids, you've seen it in others you know. You can probably even recognize it in yourself. It's common to all of us at one time or another.

In our story from 2 Kings 6, we see it in the man who loses the ax head in the river. He wants to be part of the school of the prophets that Elisha had established. We never do learn the man's name but we can see that he's searching for significance, he wants to be picked.

The Bible never specifies how they chose those who would be students of the school but this man wanted to be a part, he wanted to belong. In his heart his cry was, "Hey, pick me!"

The school had grown and their building needed to be enlarged so a project was underway to rebuild the school using trees that were growing down by the river. But this would be a big job. The trees needed to be cut down, limbs needed to be cut off, bark needed to be stripped. This was quite an undertaking and once again the young man yearned to step up and be a part of what was going on. He didn't care what he did, he just wanted to be a part. And he got his wish. He was chosen to be on the team of builders.

Notice, he wasn't chosen because he was good-looking or because he was famous. He couldn't have been well-known or popular, his name isn't even mentioned. He wasn't chosen because of his social standing or because he was rich. In fact, he was so poor, he had to borrow an ax just to be on the crew. So, he didn't have anything. No prestige, no pedigree, no prowess, just an ache in his heart to belong. And the cry of his heart was answered. And now centuries later, we are learning lessons from his life, from his experience at the river's edge.

We also see this yearning in the life of the prophet Isaiah. In Isaiah 6:8 it says, "Also I heard the voice of the Lord, saying, Whom shall I send, and who will go for us? Then said I, Here am I; send me." Just like the man with the borrowed ax and like the boys on the playground, the cry of Isaiah's heart was, "Hey, pick me!"

One of my favorite "Pick me" stories happened when I was just ten years old. A man named Don Pfeifer was preaching in a little church up in McArthur, Ohio. Now I admired Don Pfeifer even as a young boy and I loved to listen to him preach so when my older sister said, "I'm going to go listen to Don Pfeifer preach tonight" I quickly replied, "I'm going with you!" This was my sister Kathy, who is ten years older than I am. So she was twenty, I was ten.

I remember, we were the only ones in the family who went to church that night. At one point in his sermon, Don stopped. And to my ten-year-old mind, it seemed like he looked straight at me. I could feel his stare. He said, "If anybody here feels like they're called to preach or called specifically to do something for the Lord, I just want you to come up and talk to me after the service."

I felt a hot rush come over my face. I felt so convicted that he was speaking to me, I couldn't wait for the sermon to be over so I could go down and talk with him. Just about as soon as he said, "Amen" to his closing prayer, I was up out of the pew and going down the aisle to talk to him.

We sat down together on the front row of pews and he talked to me about all kinds of things. Now remember, I was only ten years old but he spoke to me like I was much older, much more mature. Then he talked to me about the gift of preaching.

Don Pfeifer lit a fire of desire inside me that night. I went home with one thought in mind, *I want to be a preacher!* Little did either of us dream that exactly twenty years later, I would take over as the pastor of his church and become his pastor. To this day I don't know what he saw in me as a little ten-year-old boy but he picked me out of all those folks to talk to that night. And I'm sure glad he did.

Picked for Celebrity or Significance?

I'll be honest. When I was a kid on the playground, I wanted to be picked for the team so I could be somebody and maybe, just maybe if I could kick a home run I could be a hero, a playground celebrity if only for a short while. Many of us want to be picked, but for all the wrong reasons. Sure, we want God to use us but we hope He uses us in these ways and not those ways. Sadly, many of us would choose celebrity over significance.

Significance says, "You don't need to know my name. I'm anonymous," while celebrity cries out, "I need to be noticed! Pick me for the most famous post, most financially rewarding, most regarded, or most widely seen." Instead, our heart's cry should be, "Pick me, Lord, for Your purposes."

I'm the pastor of a church and I've seen it time and time again over the course of my lifetime. People come to church wondering what they can get instead of what they can give. They cry, "Hey, pick me!" but for all the wrong reasons. They may volunteer for certain positions because it would put them up front in the limelight where people can notice them. They simply want the recognition and the fanfare, the position or the title.

People like this may be saying, "Hey, pick me," but there's always the qualifier, "What exactly are you going to pick me for?" They think, "I'd be more than happy to have the microphone and be on the platform Sunday morning to make announcements, to preach or help with the worship team and maybe sing a solo."

But when God says, "I picked you to work in the nursery. Or to help stack chairs, or park cars, or clean the building" it's quite a different story. "Hey, pick me" turns quickly into, "I hope he doesn't choose me!"

Picked to Play Harmonica

I remember one fellow that the Lord picked in such a profound way; he's made a significant imprint on my life, even though I don't remember his name. I first remember meeting him because he was a janitor in our school when I was a kid. Today, I suppose we would call him a custodian. He was a nice old man and would take the time out of his day to talk to us kids and get to know us. I remember the way he treated us kids. He was warm, engaging, and friendly.

When I got older, I learned that when he was a young man he had served as a paratrooper during World War II. As a kid it was hard for me to imagine this little old man, frail as ever, jumping out of airplanes. From my perspective, working at the school was probably what he'd done his whole life. But this man had survived all four years of the war and came back home and started working at the school.

I remember, years later after I started preaching, I was invited to preach a revival at the old Zion Number Three Church. The first time I walked in the building, this little old man was one of the first faces I recognized. He had been a member of that church all along.

Now in those days, many churches back in those hills had the tradition of "opening the floor," that is, they'd give others the chance to share a testimony or sing a song or read a scripture. Every service was open mic.

At a certain time in the service the pastor would ask, "Does anyone have a testimony? Anyone want to give the devil a black eye? Who wants to share what the Lord has done for you? Anyone have a song? Anybody?"

From time to time people would pop up and share what was on their hearts with the gathered congregation. The time I was there to preach they asked the question to the crowd, "Does anyone have something they'd like to share?" I looked out from my place at the front and saw that little old retired custodian stir in his seat. He was probably well over seventy years old by then and he'd sat quietly the whole service until now.

He raised one hand while reaching in his pocket with the other. He slowly stood up and pulled out an old harmonica. He put it to his mouth and began to play an old church song, sweet and low. He didn't even play that well but this was an old hymn that everyone knew and this was a very forgiving audience. The sound of that harmonica filled the church and changed the entire atmosphere of the room. People began to weep as the presence of the Lord descended down upon us.

Here was a guy who'd jumped out of airplanes as a young man but had spent the rest of his days cleaning up messes that the elementary students had made around the school. That night, the Lord didn't pick him to preach or to sing or to do some grand thing. But He did pick him for a purpose, and that purpose was to stand and play Amazing Grace on his old harmonica. And God used him and his gift to change the whole atmosphere in that church.

You may think that's no big deal, that there's nothing particularly significant or powerful about playing a harmonica in church. But I was impacted by that man as I'm sure many others were. And I continue to be impacted by his story. I'm here today telling you about him many years later, even though I don't even remember his name.

You may be reading this now and feeling that familiar tug at your heart. Maybe you didn't play the harmonica in church but God picked you for something else. Maybe you gave of yourself in some other way. Maybe you quietly gave money to the local homeless shelter or gave a hug to someone in need of a human touch or you told someone that Jesus loves them. The cry of your heart was, "Hey, pick me!" and God answered that prayer. He picked you and you changed the atmosphere because of your willingness to give your gift.

Picked to Sing

God will always answer the prayer of a heart that's crying, "Hey, pick me." And sometimes the ones He picks are unexpected. I remember well an experience I had when I was just a boy going to camp. Now I need to tell you, this wasn't "summer camp" like you may think of today with zip lines, white water rafting, bonfires at night and camp craft classes during the day.

No, these were old-fashioned "camp meetings." Our camp meetings were usually about ten days long, with powerful services in a huge tent tabernacle with wooden benches to sit on and sawdust thrown down to cover the ground. I remember on the last Sunday of camp they would always do something called a "Song Fest." This was a service where we'd all meet in the tent and sing the old hymns together. But it was also a time where folks could sign up to sing specials in front of the congregation, some in a group and some as a solo performance.

You need to understand, not everyone who signed up was a gifted singer. Some, far from it! But they were willing to share their gift of song with the rest of us and we were a friendly crowd and recognized them for their willingness to give. Plus, we knew almost everyone there and pulled for them to do well.

But some of these presentations were really spectacular. The music would swell and our hearts would lift. The Holy Spirit would fall in that tent and we'd be carried away by His anointing. But over time, the thrill of this kind of experience began to wane. The music was still very good but there didn't seem to be the powerful anointing like there once was. The music would swell like before and we'd all stand to our feet and raise our hands, but it was like we were just going through the motions. It was all human effort and no anointing.

So one year the organizers decided to shake things up a little and stop doing the Song Fest. They didn't make the change because all of a sudden they decided that they didn't want to feel the anointing or experience the spectacular. Their decision wasn't because they didn't like the individuals or the groups who got up to sing. Many of them were very talented and did a great job. They decided to make the change because it just wasn't like it used to be.

So on the last Sunday of camp meeting there was a service but no Song Fest. When they were getting ready to draw to a close, Dr. Tipton stood up to close with a word of prayer. He was at the pulpit before a congregation of around 1,200 people, maybe more. And right down front on the very first row sat a little old lady. I don't remember her name but she sat down front in the same place every service. I was just a kid but I enjoyed talking to her throughout the week of camp meeting.

Just before Dr. Tipton closed in prayer, she raised her little hand and in her feeble voice she said, "Dr. Tipton?" He looked down from the podium and responded kindly, "Yes, Sister." She said, "Before you close things down, could I sing a song?" And reluctantly . . . he said, "Yes."

Well, this was a big tabernacle and it seemed to take forever for her to make her way to the front. She had a cane in each hand and carefully put one foot in front of the other on that sawdust floor. Finally, a couple men helped her up the wooden steps and across the massive platform. She placed her two canes on the modesty rail and slowly made her way to the pulpit.

She looked so small and feeble on that massive platform. The little old woman took hold of that pulpit on either side to hold herself steady. Then she braced herself and reared back and began to sing with all the strength her old body could muster.

Starting out, there was nothing spectacular about it, no accompaniment or unique instrumentation. Just a simple lyric sung with a feeble but full, confident voice. But I want to tell you something, that day the Lord picked her. I was just a kid but I knew from the moment she started singing that this was something special.

I don't know the title of the song she sang but way back in the recesses of my memory I recall the first two lines,

> *"I came to Him the first time for salvation*
> *He did not fail me then.*
> *I came to Him the second time for the baptism of the Spirit*
> *He did not fail me then."*

It's been so long ago now that I don't remember the rest of that old song. But it was all about how the Lord did not fail her. I'm telling you, the glory of the Lord filled that tabernacle and as she sang her voice grew stonger, buoyed by the voices of the congregation as they joined in. The people of God began to shout. Hundreds made their way to the aisle and began to pour to the altar to pray. It was powerful, just powerful.

Again, this isn't to say that the spectacular is wrong or that God never wants us to perform a dramatic production of any kind. All I'm saying is that in that service on that day the cry of that woman's heart was, "Hey, pick me." And God picked her simple offering. Oh boy, did He ever! To this day it's one of strongest moves of God I've ever experienced.

God longs to respond to the willing heart, especially when that heart is willing to do whatever God asks. How many of us want to be picked but we don't have the courage to stand and play the harmonica or get up in front of a huge crowd and begin to sing?

Many of us desperately want to be picked but our desire is to be picked to do the big thing, the spectacular thing, the thing that will be noticed, to kick the ball perfectly and get the home run. We want celebrity instead of signicifance. But as you know, God's ways are not man's ways. And He doesn't care about celebrity. He will often pick us to do the unexpected, unplanned, and impromptu thing.

The man with the ax was nobody special. He was so poor he had to borrow an ax just to be a part of the team. But the cry of his heart was genuine. He wanted to do whatever he could to be chosen by God and if that meant swinging an ax, he was all in.

God created each of us on purpose for purpose. He has a plan for each one of us to fulfill. He's just waiting on us to make ourselves available to Him with no reservations. He wants to hear our heart's cry of "Hey, pick me!"

6

God's Sovereign Selection

We know that God longs to hear our heart's cry of "Hey, pick me!" We know He wants to choose us on purpose for a purpose. But what happens when we've cried out, "Hey, pick me!" and we've finally been chosen for significance but something goes wrong, and we end up making a mess of things?

We had our chance, our window of opportunity but we missed out or messed up in some way. Because of our failure, we believe ourselves to be benched and no longer worthy of being chosen. And yet, even in the midst of all that, God reaches down and forgives us and says, "I still choose YOU!"

Let me take the opportunity right now to remind you that no matter what you've done in your past, you are not disqualified. When you ask God for His forgiveness, He not only forgives you, He forgets your sin . . . completely! You are not benched. You are not defined by your sin or by your past. God sees through all that ugliness, and He continues to choose you for His purposes going forward.

You don't have to be a Bible scholar to recognize that it's God's nature to choose the undesirable, the unqualified, the unnoticed, or the one who seems so unlikely. Just think about all the examples from scripture where God defies the understanding of man and selects the unexpected. I like to say that He exercises His "Sovereign Selection."

Remember the story of Moses? He was Hebrew but by divine appointment grew up in the palace of Pharaoh. When he learned of his true ancestry, he attempted to free the slaves in his own way by using his own strength to kill an Egyptian and then try to cover up his crime by burying him in the sand. But he was so fearful of Pharaoh's wrath that he fled to the back side of the desert and stayed there for forty years.

I'm sure there were many times sitting on the mountainside watching over the sheep that he thought back on how far he'd fallen, consumed by regret. In Egypt, he was considered a prince with riches beyond compare, servants at his beck and call, and armies awaiting his command.

Now, because he'd allowed his anger to get the best of him, the only thing he ruled over was a bunch of sheep. God had picked him, but he messed up and missed his chance and lost his window of opportunity. He was destined to spend the rest of his life in the desert, and the only army he commanded wore wool coats!

And yet . . .

Don't you love the "and yets" of the Bible? Those times when God sees us in our sin and shame and forgives us. He restores us and selects us even though we don't feel worthy. We consider ourselves disqualified, but God chooses us anyway and gives us new purpose, direction, and significance. Now, when God appeared to Moses in the burning bush, He was very clear about His purpose. Things would be done in His way, under His anointing, and in His strength. And this time Moses was ready.

Have you felt like Moses? Like you've messed things up too much? Have you ever thought that you've lost your chance and that God will never put His hand on you again? My friend, nothing could be further from the truth. God is not through with you . . . not by a long shot! He is the Redeemer! And He will restore you and choose you for a purpose. He will bring significance to your life!

That's what Sovereign Selection is all about. The word "sovereign" means having supreme rank, power, or authority. In other words, sovereign means you can do whatever you want because no one outranks you. That's what God does with us. He retains the right to act as He wishes. He's not limited to our understanding or perspective. His choices don't have to make sense to us. He can choose the unlikely, select the unqualified, and pick the unworthy if He wants.

Of course, the reason He does this is that He knows us, He knows our nature. He knows that if there's any way at all, we'll take all the credit for His accomplishments! If we believe we're worthy enough or that we deserve to be picked, we'll take the glory when the plan succeeds.

On the other hand, if we know we're not smart enough, or creative enough, or strong enough or rich enough to succeed and yet through God, we achieve anyway . . . then all the glory goes to Him. We know there's no way we could have succeeded on our own.

It's easy to look through the Bible and see the times when God used His "Sovereign Selection." We looked at how it occurred in the life of Moses. But it also happened in the lives of Esther and Ruth, Gideon, Noah, Peter, Paul, and many others. God's Sovereign Selection was evident on the day the shepherd boy David was anointed to be king of Israel.

Man Looks at the Outside, but God Looks at the Heart

One of my favorite stories from scripture about Sovereign Selection has to be from I Samuel 16 . . .

God spoke to the prophet Samuel telling him, "I'm going to anoint a new king." He said, "I want you to get yourself down to Jesse's house in Bethle-hem." So Samuel makes his way down to Jesse's house. He's got a brand-new flask of oil that he's been saving to pour over the head of the man God chooses to be king. The current king is Saul, but by this time he's been rejected by God. So Samuel welcomes this word from God and says to himself, "God has a new king in mind and he's at Jesse's house in Bethlehem."

So Samuel shows up and says to Jesse, "God sent me to your house. I've got the oil. Today we're going to anoint one of your sons to become the new king over God's people."

Of course, you can imagine how Jesse feels. He's one proud papa and can barely contain himself! This is a life-changing event! The prophet has come to his house to anoint the new king! He's excited and proud. So, he fetches his sons and brings them before the prophet Samuel so he can choose the right one to be king.

I imagine Jesse getting the most elegant chair in the house and setting it in the middle of the room for Samuel to sit in and then parading his sons through one at a time to stand before the old prophet. The first one in is Eliab, Jesse's oldest boy. Samuel thinks to himself, *"Surely this will be the one the Lord wants as our next king! He's the oldest son. Why this young man even looks like a king to me!"*

But God quickly tells Samuel, "Quit looking at his outward appearance! I have rejected this one to be king." And then God reminded him, "I don't look at the things people look at. People get distracted by the outward appearance, but I look at the heart." So Samuel shook his head and sent Eliab out of the room and called for Jesse's next son.

So Jesse sent Abinadab in to pass by in front of the prophet but Samuel said, "The Lord hasn't chosen this one either." Then came Shammah, Nethanel, Raddaai, and Ozem. But God rejected each one of them as well. Samuel looked at Jesse and said, "Are you sure these are all your sons?"

Now the *King James Version* of the Bible says, "Again, Jesse made seven of his sons to pass before Samuel . . . " (1 Samuel 16:10). So it looks like they repeated the process one more time to make sure. But again, God rejected each of them. So Samuel says, "Jesse, I'm sure God sent me here to your house to anoint one of your sons. Are these all your boys? Are you sure you don't have any more?"

Jesse says, "Well, there's still the youngest. He's out in the pasture keeping the sheep." I know this story well and have preached from this passage hundreds of times over the years, and it still baffles me. How would you feel if the prophet showed up to your house to anoint the next king and you're not even considered? Your father parades all your brothers by in front of the prophet . . . and then does it again before saying, "Oh yeah, there's the youngest boy out in the field."

Talk about taking a hit to your confidence! Your dad says, "Nah, God wouldn't want to choose David to be king." Jesse doesn't even consider his youngest son David, and it doesn't even cross his mind that David may be the one.

David was overlooked. And not just overlooked, he was ignored by his dad! His own father left him outside. Finally, Jesse admits to Samuel, "Well, there's little David out there in the pasture." Samuel tells Jesse to bring him in.

Now can you imagine the scene? David comes in from watching the sheep. He has no idea what's going on. All his brothers are standing around dejected in the front room. David is called to the back of the house to stand in front of the old prophet. This is the big moment . . .

And God tells Samuel, "This is the one! I choose him! You all had your own ideas about who would be king, but this is MY SOVEREIGN SELEC-TION!" God told Samuel, "Lay your hand on him and pour the anointing oil over him! Anoint this boy to be the next king!"

God chooses the one He wants even though it makes no sense in the natural. I can imagine Jesse standing there watching his son being anointed to be king thinking, *"Really? David? Is he the one? I sure would've never figured that!"* But David was the one. That's the way God chooses! He doesn't look at the outside . . . He looks at the heart.

Created on Purpose

Think of Jesus making the choices of men who would become His disci-ples. He walked the sandy shores of the Sea of Galilee. He walked past all those boats shoved up on the beach, full of crews of men working to get their catch ready for market. But Jesus zeroes in on three guys. He sees James, John, and Peter and He chooses them. There were many, many others out there that day and yet these are the ones He decided to follow Him.

What was it about those three guys that resonated in Jesus, that made Him call out to them, "Follow Me"? Was it a look in their eyes or the color of their clothes? Was it how diligently they were working? No, it was simply God's Sovereign Selection. Jesus chose them because they were the ones God had chosen.

I'm a pastor, and every single time I have the honor of dedicating a child, I cradle that baby in my arms. As a church family, we pray over and anoint that child, dedicating him or her to God's service. I look down at that little one and say, "You are created on purpose and with purpose."

I don't doubt that David's brothers were the same way; they were created on purpose and with purpose. It's just that their purpose didn't happen to be king of Israel. But God, in His sovereignty, placed one brother here in this place and another brother there in that place, putting each one in the place they were created to be.

I'm reminded of Saul who later became Paul and wrote two-thirds of the New Testament. He was a very educated man, a scholar. He spent his early adulthood as a leader in the temple, studying in the great halls of learning of that day.

Saul was a skilled leader and an incredible orator. I think he had the potential to end his life as a philosopher, much like Socrates or Aristotle. He certainly had the skills to become a strong military leader. But God had other plans for him. While Saul was busy building his own reputation, God was working in the background preparing Saul for a different purpose, a different plan.

God sovereignly chose Saul, even though it made no sense at all. He reached down on that dusty road to Damascus and knocked Saul off his horse, blinded him and said, "I choose YOU!" God literally knocked Saul off his high horse. He humbled Saul and threw him in the dirt and called him into a whole new purpose, something far more significant than Saul could have ever imagined.

I like the old quote, "God doesn't call the qualified. He qualifies the called." God doesn't pick the likely or the obvious. He loves to take the most unlikely candidate and put him or her in a place of significance to influence his or her world.

The Story of Old Johnny Brown

When I was in college, I remember an old man who came to speak in one of our chapel services. In his sermon, he told the story about when he was a young pastor, fresh out of seminary, and even though he was from the north, they sent him down south to a little country church.

The old preacher continued his story, "When I pulled into town I went straight to the general store where I knew there'd be a crowd of people. Sure enough, the parking lot was full. I walked in the store and announced, 'Hello folks, I just wanted to introduce myself. I'm the new preacher down at the church.'

And they said, "Welcome, preacher! Welcome to the community! It's good to have you. But we have a question for you. Is old Johnny Brown going to be allowed to come to your church?" Having no idea who Johnny Brown was, I quickly responded, "He sure is! Anyone's allowed to come to church. As far as I'm concerned the Gospel is for everybody. I don't know who old Johnny Brown is, but he's welcome at my church anytime."

Well, it didn't take me long to learn that old Johnny Brown was a strange man indeed. He could not form words with his mouth. The only way he could communicate was by loud outbursts of grunting and yelling. And of course, because he was so strange, he had never been accepted into the community though he'd lived there all his life.

He lived in a clapboard shack down by the edge of town. He dressed in an old brown coat with a ratty collar he pulled up high on his neck. He wore a beat up hat that he pulled down low on his head almost hiding his face from view. To make matters worse, he never bathed or washed his clothes. You knew he was coming because his smell would hit you before you could see him. Over the years he'd become an object of ridicule among the folks of this small town.

It was on one of those first Sunday mornings that I pulled up to the church and noticed that a bunch of the elders and a couple of deacons were sitting on the front steps waiting for me. As I approached they said, "Preacher, the word on the street is that old Johnny Brown is coming to church today." I told them, "The man is welcome in this church. I won't turn him away."

About halfway through the second song the doors at the back banged open and into the church walked old Johnny Brown. The folks in the pews were restless, uneasy, and didn't know what to do. He stunk to high heaven, so the ushers got him a chair and made him sit all the way in the back, in the corner by himself.

I did my best to preach that morning, but it was tough to stay focused. I was interrupted often by Johnny Brown's outbursts from the back. I didn't know if he was agreeing or disagreeing with me. I wasn't even sure if he could understand what I was trying to say. But I preached the Gospel. I told about how Jesus gave His life as a ransom for our sin and when I gave the altar call, to my shock . . . and dismay, old Johnny Brown came walking down the aisle to kneel at the altar.

I saw him coming and offered up a quick prayer to God. "Lord, how in the world am I going to minister to this man? How is he even going to be able to say the sinner's prayer if he can't form the words? Lord, what am I going to do?"

Just that quick the Lord said to me, "You don't need words to share the Gospel. Tell him the story in a way he'll understand." So, I grabbed my Bible from off the pulpit and went down to the altar and put my hand on the back of his scruffy, dirty neck.

I looked down at him and shook the Bible in his face and shouted, "Jesus died," and I pointed to the cross on the wall at the front of the church. "He died for you on a cross!" I took my Bible and shoved it in front of him and pounded the Bible on his chest. "And Johnny Brown, He wants to live in your heart!" I did that over and over, "Jesus died on the cross" and I'd point to the cross. "And He wants to live in your heart!" and I'd pound the Bible on his chest. Over and over again I proclaimed that simple Gospel message to old Johnny Brown as he knelt at the altar. I had no idea whether it was getting through to him or not.

A few weeks went by and I hadn't seen or heard anything about old Johnny Brown since the Sunday he'd come to church. One morning I went up to the general store, and when I walked in, I asked the folks in there if they'd heard from Johnny Brown. They said, "Every morning he walks up toward the interstate with a big ax slung over his shoulder. In the evenings he walks back down to his shack. We don't know where he's going or what he's doing."

I thought, *"I've got to figure out what's going on."* So, I got in my car and drove up toward the interstate, and when I got there and rounded the bend, I was blown away from what I saw. Up there on the hillside facing the interstate, old Johnny Brown had taken his ax and cleared the trees away. Then he'd used some of those trees to build three crosses, and he planted them in the clearing he'd made with that ax.

In front of me, I saw old Johnny Brown on the interstate stopping traffic for miles. He'd go up to each car and yank the driver's door open, take his Bible, point it at the crosses he'd fashioned and then pound that Bible to the driver's chest and yell just like I did when he came down to the altar at church.

The old preacher said, "Years later I told that story at a huge conference where I was preaching. After my sermon, a handsome couple in their mid-fifties came up to me. They told me that they'd always wondered who that guy was. The woman said, 'You see, we were on the interstate that day. That fella stopped us. He came around and pulled my husband out of the car and pointed to those rugged crosses up on the hillside and then pounded my husband's chest with that big Bible of his. He was grunting and yelling . . . we had no idea what he was trying to say.

"'We drove on down the road two or three miles and something came over both of us right there in the car. We began to weep. We were shaking and trembling. We didn't know what to do. We'd never been in church before and we couldn't explain what was going on.

"'We decided to pull the car over and get out because my husband was having a tough time driving. We staggered over to the guardrail and used it as an altar as we knelt and prayed. We said, Lord, whatever that man was telling us we need, we want it. Will You please give it to us?'"

"She said, 'We both had promising careers in the medical field but gave them up for the Gospel that day. A few weeks later we answered the call to go and preach the Gospel. Since then God has sent us around the world establishing hospitals and medical clinics. We've had the opportunity to pray with thousands of people to receive Jesus Christ into their hearts. Across this planet, there have been thousands of people who are saved and healed today because old Johnny Brown stopped our car and pressed his big old Bible on our hearts.'"

Listen to me, by His Sovereign Selection, God can take a smelly old man who couldn't even talk and change the world and lead thousands of people to Him. He chose old Johnny Brown to leave a stamp of significance on this earth because of what he did by the power of Christ to change lives by the thousands all across this world.

It's not about being qualified or worthy. It's not about being rich or good-looking. God's Sovereign Selection often makes no earthly sense. It doesn't have to. But His choices will always result in Him getting all the credit. He chooses us and anoints us to make a difference in this world.

You may not feel worthy or capable of doing what God has called you to do, but that doesn't matter. He called you for a purpose and He will give you whatever you need to accomplish that purpose for His glory. By Sovereign Selection He chose YOU!

7

Joining the Cause— Stepping Into Your Purpose

A Cause Is . . .

The dictionary definition of the word "cause" is "a principle, ideal, goal, or movement to which a person or group is dedicated." In other words, a "cause" is the answer to the WHY question. Why are you doing what you're doing? Why are you living where you're living? Why did you choose the career you've chosen? In fact, a common answer to any WHY question often begins with the word, "beCAUSE . . . . " But a cause is so much more than just the reason for doing something.

A cause is your motivation to get up in the morning. It's the deep down desire to keep on going even when things get tough. A cause urges you onward even when others have long ago given up. A cause can be intensely personal, inspiring you, giving you dreams and visions for a whole new world, a world that you want to create for you and your family or others. A cause is a higher calling, a craving for significance.

But do people always need causes or reasons to do things? After more than thirty years in ministry, I've seen firsthand that the sad answer to that question is no, they don't. Many people are floating through this life, living without a cause. They have no purpose, no calling, and no cause. Their entire life is merely a reaction to what is happening to them in the moment. They do nothing for cause; they react to things, whether positive or negative.

They need to eat, so they get a job. They need warmth and shelter, so they rent a place to live. The things they do in life are just reactions to the things they are feeling or experiencing in some way. A cause does not motivate them; they're just doing what they think they need to do to survive another day. The only reason some people live the life they do is to get by.

Whatever happened to passion and purpose? To destiny or calling? These are the causes that we live for, the reasons to work hard at a job or live in a particular community. Many folks may pay rent on a place to live, but it's not a home. It's not a place to live, only a place to stay until something else comes along.

Let me challenge you with this question . . . why have you chosen the occupation you have today? Is there more than a reason? Is there a cause beyond a paycheck or insurance benefit? My wife is a teacher in the local school. She's a strong, smart woman and could have had her choice of many different professions but if you were to ask her why she's chosen to be a schoolteacher, she could answer by pointing to her salary. She has a master's degree, so she makes a fair amount, and that's certainly a blessing to our family. She could also point to the generous health plan provided by the school district. Thank God for that. Our family is blessed with good health care.

These are good reasons, but what about the cause? The cause that keeps her showing up every day is the little girl in one of her classes whose daddy just got put in prison. The little girl's momma is addicted to meth, so she's been taken from the home and placed in the foster care system.

Her cause is a little boy in her class. My wife got a letter the other day from a woman who wrote, "You've changed my little boy's life. I don't know how to thank you. You've made such a difference in his life. You've blessed our whole family because of the way you've blessed his life." My wife's students are her cause. They are the wind in her sails, the cables that pull her through each day.

You see, the cause will always outweigh the reason. I'm not saying that my wife would work for nothing or give up her health care but what I am saying is that when she's focused on her students, her cause for teaching, she's not as worried about how much she makes or what her benefits package looks like.

Sure, a job can meet a need but does it really scratch that deep down itch for significance that only a cause can reach? If you're striving to live a life of significance, "just getting by" is never going to be enough. That deep down itch will never get scratched. Sadly too many people, in fact, too many Christians are living lives without a cause.

What about you? How can you tell if you're living for a cause or not? People who have no cause in their lives are pushed around aimlessly, randomly by the circumstances of their lives. Sound familiar?

If a cause is the thing to which you are dedicated, it becomes the goal, the motivation that gets you up out of bed in the morning. The cause is what draws you; it not only pulls you through your day, it pulls you through your life.

A Cause Worth Dying For

There's a famous letter written by Sullivan Ballou back during the early months of the Civil War. Major Ballou fought for the Union in the 2nd Rhode Island Infantry. In a letter to his wife, he gives us a great example of what I'm talking about. You should have no trouble picking out causes he lives for. He wrote, "Sarah, my love for you is deathless. It seems to bind me with mighty cables, that nothing but Omnipotence can break; and yet, my love of country comes over me like a strong wind, and bears me irresistibly on with all those chains, to the battlefield."

Major Ballou is actually speaking here of two causes that he's living for, fighting for, and prepared to die for in the Civil War. His first cause is the love that he has for his wife, Sarah. He describes that cause as "mighty cables" that bind him together with her and their boys. But then he says that his love of country "comes over him like a strong wind" pulling him irresistibly toward the battlefield. His love of country was his second cause.

As you read his words, it's easy to see that Major Ballou's causes were so much higher than just reasons why he got married or why he chose to join the Union army. These causes and the way he describes them are strong cables that pulled him through his life, charting his course and helping him make the choices he needed to make. That's the power of living life on purpose, living for a cause . . . and dying for a cause. You see, Major Sullivan Ballou was struck and killed as the Rhode Islanders advanced from Matthews Hill in the First Battle of Manassas just a week after he wrote this letter.

I love the picture of a great cause that his letter paints in our minds. Just like Major Ballou, your cause is a strong wind that fills your sails and pulls your ship through the sea. Without wind, a sailboat drifts according to whatever current might be pulling it along. It's aimless, directionless, like a ping-pong ball floating on the sea, which is an accurate description of a life lived without purpose.

The apostle Paul said it like this in Ephesians 4:14, "That we henceforth be no more children, tossed to and fro, and carried about with every wind of doctrine, by the sleight of men, and cunning craftiness, whereby they lie in wait to deceive." Paul is encouraging us in this passage to live life on purpose for a cause.

Our man in 2 Kings 6 had a cause worth living for. He wanted to be a part of the school of the prophets. Along with the other student prophets present, they wanted to build a larger school to meet the needs of their growing enrollment. They tried to influence generations. That was their cause, and the man wanted to participate so strongly that he borrowed an ax so he could join them.

Is There a Cause?

By the time the shepherd boy David arrived at the Philistine battlefront in the valley of Elah, the prophet Samuel had already anointed him to be king of Israel. He was still a boy and wasn't ready yet to assume the throne. He still had much to learn about leadership and the ways of the Lord. But his heart was pure, and it was dedicated to God and His purposes.

David's father Jesse comes to him and says, "Your brothers are down there serving an important cause with King Saul. They're fighting the Philistines. I mixed up some fried chicken and some nice taters, and I want you to take some down there for them to eat. They need their strength."

Of course, I'm paraphrasing here, but it seems likely to me that good people have been feasting on fried chicken with taters for eons, and who knows, maybe that's what Jesse fixed for David to take to his older brothers. Back in the hills where I grew up every single Sunday after church, families would sit down to a table loaded with either fried chicken or pot roast, sometimes both! If you aimed to be a preacher, you better like one of those meals. I almost always had a craving for fried chicken, so I knew preaching was just the thing for me!

So David loads up his donkey with chicken and taters and goes down to the valley to see his brothers. They are with the rest of Saul's army tucked away, trembling in their tents fearing for their lives. Meanwhile, this colossal mammoth of a man stands in the middle of the valley defiling the name of God Jehovah. Goliath, the uncircumcised warrior, taunts and defies the armies of God and David won't have it. David says to those around him, "What's going on here? What's with you guys? You can't allow this guy to talk this way!"

David's brothers just looked at him and shook their heads. To them, he's only the youngest brother, the little shepherd boy out watching the sheep. They got mad and said, "You just go on home, you little brat. You have no idea what you're talking about. Just give us our chicken and go back to the sheep where you belong." Remember, when you are searching for purpose and significance there will always be naysayers trying to tell you where you belong.

David's brothers had had enough, and they just wanted to be rid of their baby brother. But David would have none of it. He smelled an opportunity for significance. He could feel in his bones that a moment of destiny was about to fall on his shoulders. He asked his brothers, "Wait a minute here. Is there a cause? Have you guys just given up on defending the name of our Lord? It seems to me that there's a cause here worth fighting for!" He said, "The whole reason you've come down to this valley to fight the Philistines is to defend the name of the Lord and bring Him glory. Are you going to turn your back on that cause so easily? Since there's a cause here, and none of you will go fight this giant, I'll do it. I'll fight for the cause! Let me at 'em!" (1 Samuel 17). And of course, we know the rest of the story. David stepped into his destiny, defeating the giant and fixing his reputation as an unlikely overcomer in the minds and hearts of millions of folks down through history.

Nehemiah's Cause

There's another excellent story from scripture about Nehemiah. He was exiled in Persia and had heard from others that the walls of Jerusalem had fallen and lay in ruins. He wept aloud. His holy city was destroyed and laid waste. Rebuilding the walls of Jerusalem became his cause, his reason to get up in the morning. He planned and strategized for just the right way to approach the king of Persia with his urgent request.

He convinced the king to allow him to return to Jerusalem with some others and spearhead a project to rebuild those walls. This cause was difficult beyond imagination. Not only did the reconstruction of the walls present enormous challenges; they had to fight off (literally!) opposition by carrying weapons in one hand and their tools in the other.

It was during a particularly difficult moment when he was urged to stop his work and come down to meet with some "so-called" friends. Nehemiah simply replied, "I sent messengers unto them, saying, I am doing a great work, so that I cannot come down: why should the work cease, whilst I leave it, and come down to you?" (Nehemiah 6:3).

In other words, Nehemiah was much too consumed with his cause to meet with those who meant him ill. I love that. "I am doing a great work, so that I cannot come down." That's the power of a cause! It keeps us focused and moving forward.

We are created of God and then redeemed by God for the cause of bringing Him glory. Wherever He puts us, there's a cause. If you're a part of a church, there's a cause. If you're part of a family, there's a cause. Whatever you are a part of, wherever you have been called, there's a cause. If you're part of a team, you have a cause. There's always a cause, something great to strive for, to live for.

The Cause of Christ

My dad was a World War II vet, and he used to say to me, "Son, I want you to remember something. There's always going to be things in this world worth living for and things worth dying for." This statement may seem obvious if you were raised like I was, but the truth is, you don't hear people talking about that kind of thing much anymore.

I've always remembered those words; "There are things worth living for and things worth dying for." When you ask Jesus to come into your heart and promise to live for Him, you adopt the Cause of Christ. He is worth living for! And He is worth dying for. The apostle Paul said it this way, "For to me to live is Christ, and to die is gain" (Philippians 1:21).

So, is there a cause, one worth living for, one worth dying for? Absolutely! I believe there's a tremendous cause discovered in the unveiling of Christ and the unmasking of our own delusion.

What does that mean? To unveil Christ is to help others discover who Jesus is. As ministers of the Gospel, that's our cause . . . to pull back the veil and reveal the true Jesus as the risen Savior. When Jesus appeared to

Thomas with the other disciples in the upper room after His crucifixion, Jesus pulls aside His robe to reveal the spear marks in His side. He raises the sleeves of His robe to show the scarred hands. In a sense, Jesus pulled back the veil to reveal His true self, the Lamb who was slain. And Thomas believed. When people see Jesus as the Savior He truly is . . . they believe in Him.

That's the first part of the Cause of Christ, to reveal Him to a dark and lost world. What's the other part? To unmask our delusion. Not only do we need the world to understand who Jesus is, but we also need to take a hard look at who we are. We are lost. We are sinners in need of a Savior. We're deluded to think we can do it on our own. In Peter's case, once he understood who he was, he knew he was unworthy to be hung on a cross like Christ, so he insisted on being crucified upside down. Once we're able to see through our delusion, we see ourselves for who we are, and revelation comes.

The Cause of Christ for the Church is to peel back the robe and reveal Jesus for who He is, the Savior to a lost world. And to trade in the mask of who we think we are in favor of who we are with no mask at all. This is our cause! It's our reason for living. This cause, like mighty cables, pulls us forward when times get tough. It's what gets us out of bed in the morning even when we feel that no one understands or that the world is against us.

If you're living without a cause, you are living an empty existence, merely reacting to life happening around you. As Paul said, you are tossed to and fro, carried about with every wind of doctrine. But the Cause of Christ will put wind in your sails and draw you ever closer to your destiny of significance. It's time for you to join the Cause!

8

It's Bigger Than Me— The Sign of a Worthy Cause

A Work in Progress . . . for Generations!

Rising over 560 feet from downtown Barcelona, Spain, are the towers of the cathedral "Sagrada Familia." This ambitious project broke ground on March 19, 1882 . . . and it's not yet finished! The building is only a little over 70 percent completed and not scheduled to be finished until 2026.

The chief architect when the project began was a man named Antoni Gaudi and when people used to ask him why the project was taking so long, Gaudi just looked at them and said, "My client is not in a hurry." Of course, he was talking about God.

What drives generations of builders, designers, architects, and laborers of all skill levels to continue to work on such a project knowing they will never see it completed? It's because they've committed themselves to a cause that's much bigger than they are, much bigger than just what they can accomplish on their own. They have embraced the fact that they are laboring now on something that only those not yet born will be able to enjoy fully.

The truth is, the bigger the cause, the more powerful its pull. Often the cause, by its sheer size and tidal pull, can be just the thing that motivates and inspires you to move forward no matter what the odds.

The Hall of Faith

Hebrews 11 contains what many refer to as "The Hall of Faith." It's a list of heroes from the Bible who had unbelievably strong faith. It's a powerful piece of scripture that causes me to well up with tears just reading it. Over and over it lists the names of these spiritual giants. By faith Abel . . . , by faith Enoch . . . , by faith Noah . . . , by faith Abraham . . . , Isaac, Jacob, Sarah, Moses, and many others.

But the part of the chapter that challenges me is found in verse 13. "These all died in faith, not having received the promises, but having seen them afar off, and were persuaded of them, and embraced them, and confessed that they were strangers and pilgrims on the earth" (Hebrews 11:13).

It says that these men and women all died "in faith, not having received the promises . . . ." That's amazing to me. They didn't have to see the promises fulfilled to know that God was going to make good on those promises. They knew He would. They had faith that He would. That's how big and powerful their cause was . . . it was so big; it reached beyond their very lives.

That's hard for us to even relate to in the culture we live in today. Because of the Internet, we've come to expect that we can have whatever we want, whenever we want it, and we get grumpy or even angry when we don't. It seems that almost nothing can keep us from having what we want, not time nor money. This culture has convinced us that we can have what we want, and we can have it now.

We have this misguided expectation that burrows so deeply inside of us that it's tough to think about actually waiting for a reward. Working hard now for a payoff down the road is a foreign concept to many today.

Have you ever been to a Christmas tree farm to cut down a tree? Did you realize that it can take up to ten years for the first trees planted to be ready for harvest? In this world of instant gratification, it seems odd to own a farm where your first crop won't even be ready for another ten long years.

But it wasn't always this way . . . there was a time when people understood that it was going to take a long time and enormous sacrifice to get the things they wanted.

A Generation with Nothing Bigger

In Chapter 7 I quoted my dad, who was a World War II veteran, "Son, I want you to remember something. There's always going to be things in this world worth living for and things worth dying for."

I believe that with my whole heart. But like I said in Chapter 7, I believe it's an unpopular, if not unheard, notion in our culture today. To ask someone to sacrifice now for a payoff they may not even live to see seems like asking too much for many people. Whether you're talking about the cathedral that's taken generations to build or the effort to fight and win World War II or something as easy as waiting ten years to harvest a Christmas tree . . . it's the promise of those "bigger than me" causes that kept those folks moving forward, kept them believing, kept them working hard, day after day, even though they knew they might not live to see the promise fulfilled. That's a cause that's big enough to live for and big enough to die for. But it seems to me that we've recently raised two or three generations in America and given them everything to live with and nothing to live for.

I believe many kids today, especially in America, are raised in homes where the biggest, most important thing is them. There's nothing more significant, nothing more important than their needs and their desires. Nothing at all.

Parents fall into the trap of making their child feel that they are the most important thing. And even as I write that I know how that sounds. Don't we want our kids to understand how valuable and precious they are to us? Of course, we do, but not if it comes at the price of making them feel as if they were the MOST important thing.

What's the biggest thing at school? My kid. What about on the football team? My kid. What about in the neighborhood or at the park or in the classroom or the church youth group? You guessed it . . . my kid! When we create a world for our children where they are the most significant thing, we do them a great disservice.

When a child believes that he or she is the biggest, most important thing around, they'll have a terrible time later on in life believing that there is a cause that's bigger than they are that's worth fighting for. Their whole world will revolve around them and what they are feeling and what they need right now.

I know parents that have taken their kids on mission trips to third world countries not so much to help the people of those countries but to show their kids that there's a big world out there that doesn't revolve around them. For kids to come face to face with severe poverty or extreme lack is really to give them a gift they'll never forget.

Seeing how others live and the hardships they have to endure instills in them the whole idea of laying down their lives for a cause bigger than themselves. It shows them that there are significant issues out there that must be dealt with. Some causes need to be embraced that have nothing at all to do with what they want or how they feel.

Working Now with a View to the Future

Let's take another look at our man from 2 Kings 6 . . .

Here's a man chopping away, working hard on a building project. Now I don't know how many other prophets there were working at this school. But I do know that when Elisha saw Elijah taken up to Heaven fifty prophets were standing on the other side of the Jordan River (2 Kings 2:7).

The Bible mentions "the sons of the prophets." Some versions say "a company." But the number cited is fifty. So let's say that here we are sometime later and these prophets are working on a building project to increase the size of the school where they were meeting. They had to increase the size because their number had grown. So now there has to be sixty, seventy, eighty . . . we don't know how many more but we know there are more than fifty.

For the purpose of the story, let's stretch it out a little. Let's say a hundred prophets were working on the project. And here's our guy who desires significance in his life so much that he wants to be picked for the crew. The cry of his heart is, "Hey, pick me!"

This poor guy wants to help build this school, he wants to join this cause that's bigger than he is, but he doesn't have any tools. So he searches and finds someone willing to let him borrow an ax. And now he's been picked, he's got his ax, and he's out there chopping away, working feverishly because he's part of a cause that's bigger than he is.

To this guy, it doesn't matter that he's not famous or influential. It's the cause that brings him significance. He doesn't care if no one will ever even know his name. But as he stops to take a breath, he considers that for years to come when he passes by this spot he'll see people going in and out of the school studying to be a prophet in Israel. He feels a renewed strength just by thinking about being able to say, "Yeah, I helped build that school with an old borrowed ax."

It's Not About YOU

It's a pretty amazing thing to realize that you're part of a cause that's bigger than you. Right away it causes you to take your eyes off yourself and your weaknesses and your strengths because you realize it's not about you. Many people believe that the World War II generation was this country's "Greatest Generation." What was it that made them so great?

The thing that made my daddy's generation so great was that they had a keen, acute awareness that they lived in a world that was bigger than them. Their lives were defined by that war and the world they changed because they joined and committed their lives to the cause of making the world a better place. My daddy was willing to sacrifice and do without so I wouldn't have to, so I would be able to have a better life than he had.

There's a famous quote by the founding father John Adams in a letter he wrote to his wife Abigail. He writes, "I must study politics and war that my sons may have liberty to study mathematics and philosophy. My sons ought to study mathematics and philosophy, geography, natural history, naval architecture, navigation, commerce, and agriculture, in order to give their children a right to study painting, poetry, music, architecture, statuary, tapestry, and porcelain." It's precisely that kind of far-reaching multi-generational vision that's been lost in today's culture.

The Benefit of a Big Family

I came from a big family. I'm the youngest of seven kids. Where I grew up, in the hills of southeast Ohio, the towns and the farms were full of big families. I might be biased, but I believe that when you come from a big family, you learn real quick that the world doesn't revolve around you. You realize it's not all about you, that there are bigger things than what you want. Maybe what we need is the return of the big family!

Families today aren't as big as they used to be and that might be one of the reasons we're raising kids who are growing up in homes where they are treated like they are the biggest, most important thing there is.

It seems to me that when you're the only child or when there are just a couple of kids in the family that it's much easier to get the impression that it's all about you. In my case, I'm the youngest of seven kids. And even though some of them had left home because they were grown, things were still tough. My dad died when I was only thirteen, and we lived in a little cabin back in the hills. It's crazy to think about but my closet at home today is probably bigger than the two tiny bedrooms we had in that cabin . . . and I don't have that big of a closet! There were six of us living in that little old cabin.

In many families, the youngest child is usually spoiled, but believe me, I learned really quick that it wasn't all about me, it was about US. We all knew that if we were going to survive, we were all going to have to join the cause. The cause was indeed bigger than me, bigger than my mother . . . more significant than any of us individually. It was going to take us all, pulling on the same rope, in the same direction to make a go of things.

So, at thirteen I began mowing lawns and doing odd jobs for folks around town. I did this not so I could have money to spend on myself, going to the movies with my friends and not so that I could buy a specific toy or game. No. I was working so that we would have food on the table. I was always diligent to save so I could help out with the household budget.

Every week I was able to put a little money back in a sock I kept in my top drawer. My mom didn't even know I was doing it. I remember her coming to me at the end of one summer. I'd been working hard throughout the hot season. With school about to start, she said to me, "Troy, we don't have enough money for clothing, for school, or school supplies."

But I knew I had about $200 saved back in that old sock in my top drawer and I went in to get it. I brought the sock into her and put it in her hand. She looked at me with a questioning expression on her face. I said, "Would this be enough to get us all some clothing and some school supplies?" She looked at me and said, "Where'd you get this?" I told her, "I've been saving a little back all summer." "Oh," she said, "you're just like your daddy. He always put a little something back for the tough times."

My daddy grew up in difficult times and those times continued into adulthood for him. And while I wouldn't wish tough times on anyone, they do cause us to see the world a bit differently. We grow up knowing that it's not about us. We know we're not nearly as independent as we might think we are. We know that we need those around us and that those folks around us need us as well. That's what I learned by growing up in a big family.

The Current Culture of the Church

I believe that the problems we've experienced in our families of raising a self-centered generation are even spilling over to our churches. The problem with the church growth movement is that we reinforce the myth that it's all about you. The leadership of many churches find themselves repeatedly asking, "What do we have to do to satisfy the customer, appease the flesh, to do all we can not to offend those who choose to walk through the doors to our church?" We've built megachurches on the back of just that kind of thinking.

We're careful to keep a close eye on the time so our services don't run too long. We don't spend too long in worship or too long in prayer, and we're careful to keep our sermons to no more than thirty minutes. We put a coffee bar in the lobby and even stream our services online so people don't have to leave the house.

Now I'm not saying that any of these things are inherently wrong in and of themselves. These are things that do warrant a conversation. I'm just saying that if we're spending all our effort to make sure we're correctly stroking our congregations and offending nobody, we're missing the point entirely.

What are these folks, who have been made to think they're the most important thing, going to think when the preacher gets up and says the words of Christ, "If you're going to follow Me you must deny yourself, take up your cross, and follow Me" (see Matthew 16:24)? "Wait a minute? What do you mean, 'deny myself'? My whole life's always been about myself!" If we're not careful, we find ourselves running after the coaxed and coddled instead of leading the called and commanded.

Think about it. It's hard to pray "THY Kingdom come" when we really mean "MY kingdom come." Many today have been taught over a lifetime that there's nothing bigger than them. There's no cause more significant, there's no one more important. But that line of thinking runs counter to everything Jesus taught and stood for.

Rich Young Ruler

Let me give you an example from scripture. In the book of Matthew, chapter 19, a wealthy young man approaches Jesus and asks Him how he can have eternal life. Jesus tells him that he must follow the commandments. The young man replies that he's followed the commandments since he was a boy. Jesus then raises the bar. He tells the young man that he's got to sell all he has and give the money away to the poor. The Bible says that the young man "went away sorrowful: for he had great possessions" (v. 22).

Now the interesting thing here is what doesn't happen. Whenever I read through this passage, what screams out to me is that Jesus didn't chase him down. He didn't run after him saying, "Hey, wait a minute! Don't go . . . maybe I reached a little far there. I'm probably asking too much. Let's talk about it a little bit. Maybe we can negotiate!"

Jesus didn't chase after him, and He said none of those things. Jesus knew that to join His cause you have to know deep down that it's not about you being comfortable. It's not about you getting everything you want or winning a trophy just for showing up.

Belonging to His Church (capital C), joining His cause takes sacrifice and a willingness to give it all, to do whatever it takes to advance the Kingdom and give God the glory. It's hard to do that if you want your church experience to be all about your hot coffee, sitting in chairs that are cozy, singing only songs you like to sing, and listening to words that tickle your ears. No, joining the Cause of Christ requires that you see a cause bigger than just you.

"Come and Die"

Dietrich Bonhoeffer was a German theologian and pastor. In 1939 Bonhoeffer was called to enlist in the Nazi army. To follow his convictions concerning war and to save his own life, Bonhoeffer arranged an invitation to leave Germany immediately and come to America to teach theology. He stayed in the US for only twenty-six days.

Bonhoeffer had found a cause much bigger than him and could stay in this country no longer. He'd found a reason worth dying for. He returned to his native land because he believed he'd been called by God to go back. The cause, like mighty cables, drew him back across the Atlantic to Germany. Once arriving, he was arrested for treason, quickly tried, convicted, and executed by the Nazis in 1945.

What was it about Bonhoeffer that sparked this willingness to sacrifice it all for the Cause of Christ? He understood that his calling, his cause, was much bigger than he was. He realized that to know God is to obey Him. It didn't matter what he wanted or what brought him comfort or safety. He was going to follow God no matter what the costs. He knew that it wasn't about him; it was about Jesus Christ and the advancement of His Kingdom.

A clue to Bonhoeffer's commitment and devotion for the Cause of Christ is found in a quote from his book, *The Cost of Discipleship*. In it he says, "When Christ calls a man He bids him come and die." Just like with the rich young ruler, Jesus asks us to give it all, to take up our cross daily and follow Him.

Bonhoeffer knew that to truly embrace the Cause of Christ you have to believe that the cause is beyond you, it's bigger than you. He knew that he would have to die to his pride and ego and live the bigger dream, embrace the bigger cause. He had found a reason worth living for, and then he embraced the Cause worth dying for.

9

Who's In Charge?
The Divine Role
of Authority

Authority is one of the most critical things for us to understand. Before we can really begin to step out into our purpose and destiny we have to figure out who's in charge. We've got to be crystal clear on who the authority is.

Think back to our story from 2 Kings 6. Here's a man who wanted to be part of something. He was crying out, "I am here! Notice me!" He was able to find some significance even though nobody knew his name. Here's a man who said, "Hey, pick me!" And he was chosen. Here's a man who understood, "I'm part of a cause." He was a guy who knew that he was part of something bigger than himself. He looked around and could see that there was a bunch of other guys out there chopping wood. He was part of a cause and he understood that if he was going to be a part of something, there has to be someone in charge.

This need to figure out who's in charge is hard wired into us when we're born. A while back I was sitting in my chair in the living room at home and my little girl Bella, who was six at the time, came up to me along with her little sister Baylee, who was five. They wanted to go play out in the woods out behind our house and they wanted me to take them.

I said, "Listen Bella, when I was your age, I didn't need anyone to take me to go out and play. You guys go on out there; just don't go too far. I don't need to go out there with you."

You know what she asked me? She was only six years old but almost instinctively she said, "Who's in charge?" I told her, "Bella, you're the oldest, you're in charge." Her comment didn't come as a surprise to me because I knew Bella; she was a take-charge kind of girl. Immediately, she took control. She turned to her little sister and said, "Come on. We're going to play in the woods and I'm in charge!"

I think it's pretty obvious, we all want our lives to be blessed, right? I mean, we want our family to be blessed, our work to be blessed, our homes, schools, neighborhoods, cities; we want all those things to be blessed.

But did you realize that you have no hope of enjoying the blessing of God until you recognize that He's the One in charge? If you want to enjoy His blessing, you need to make sure that what you're doing follows His will and function. In short, you have to be doing what God wants you to do before you can expect to receive His blessing.

God places a high premium on authority and how we choose to handle it will determine not only where we go in life but also how far we're able to go. How we treat authority will determine everything else including the degree to which you are able to experience significance in your life.

A Valuable Lesson

My son plays football for his school team. One day I picked him up in the parking lot after practice. He opened the car door, dropped in the seat, buckled his seat belt, slammed the door, and gave a frustrated sigh. Without looking up, he said, "Coach . . . . " I knew instantly just by the tone of his voice and his body language that he was getting ready to complain about something. I knew he was going to disrespect his football coach.

Before he was even able to get another word out of his mouth, I said, "Stop right there, young man!" He said, "What did I say?" I looked my boy right in the eye; I wanted him to know just how serious I was taking this. If getting authority right is important to God, it better be important to us! I quickly decided that I was going to teach my son a lesson about authority right then and there.

I told him, "If you've got something to say about your coach, you're going to say it to the coach! If you think you're going to get in my car and dismantle and uncover and disagree and talk bad about your coach, your teacher, or any other authority in your life, you better wake up, boy. It ain't gonna happen!"

My son sheepishly said, "Well, okay. I guess I'm all right now." But I told him, "Not so fast. I don't think you are okay yet. But you will be. We're going to see your coach right now." So we got out of the car, and I took him by the hand and walked him across the field over to where the coach was standing. The coach looked up and greeted me. I looked down at my son and said, "Tell the coach the problem you're having with him. Tell him how you disagree with the way he's coaching you."

So my son proceeded to talk to his coach in a very respectful way, and the coach kindly replied to him. He was wise enough to see this for what it was, which was a valuable teachable moment for my son. He patiently told my son, "Here's why I do what I do. It may be hard for you to understand, but it's really not your job to understand it. It's your job to obey my instructions." I thanked the coach, and we got back in the car and went home.

Did I overreact? I don't think so. I believe that understanding the principle of authority and respecting that authority is vital . . . probably one of the most important things we can teach our kids. I believe that lesson was well worth the time and the effort it took to go back and have that conversation with the coach.

You see, how you handle authority is important because it's going to determine where you go in life. I remember my dad telling me very early on, "You're always going to have a boss. You'll always have someone in your life that will be an authority over you. Right now, it's me and your mom and your teachers in school. When you go off to college, it'll be the professors and the deans. When you graduate and get a job, you'll have a boss. When you drive on the roads, you'll have the police. Just know that you'll always have someone over you."

All authority comes from God. And to understand God, you must first understand His authority. If you think about it, achieving significance in this life is dependent upon submitting to and understanding His authority. We can never hope to be saved from our sin until we recognize God's authority. We can wish all day long to be picked for a cause bigger than ourselves, but we'll never be humble enough to be chosen until we recognize His authority over us.

In our illustration from 2 Kings, the young man only gets picked to help build the new school because of the authority of Elisha. In the same way, we can't be part of building a church, a community, or a family until we learn how authority works.

The problem is that I believe we've been raising a generation in America who have no regard at all for authority. And parents perpetuate this attitude every time they complain, disrespect or dismantle the authority that God has placed in our lives.

The incident with my son and his coach wasn't just something I thought up on the spot. I came by it honestly. My dad set a strong example for me to follow. He never corrected a teacher who wronged me in front of me. He would never think of undermining that teacher's authority by complaining about them in front of me. And he not only set this valuable example for me but my older brothers as well.

Honoring Authority

I remember one time after my dad had died I had a teacher in school who had it out for me. He was the gym teacher, and he was a massive mountain of a man. Now to be fair, I had it coming. I was ornery . . . just as ornery as my older brothers were when they were in school. I'll admit, I was a terrible student and did all I could to cause problems in this man's class. I disrespected him at every turn.

One day he'd had enough, and he boarded me. Of course, this was back in the day when it was much more commonplace at school for a teacher or administrator to paddle a wayward student. I wasn't too bright. I didn't just choose to disrespect any ol' teacher in the school. Oh no, I chose to disrespect a former bodybuilder who was the largest, strongest man in the school . . . by far!

I remember bending over in his office and feeling the pain as he hit me with his large paddle. He came down a second time, then a third! Then something happened, and he stopped. He'd hit me so hard, he'd broken his paddle! It was a thick board, but he broke it in half.

Inside I was grateful it was over! That boarding just about killed me, but of course, I was young and cocky and acted like it didn't even hurt. On the way out of the office, the vice principal shook my hand and said, "Way to take it like a man." Inside I was dying, but I put on a brave face and told him, "To us Ervins, that's the only way we take it!" He looked down and just laughed. He'd known all my older brothers when they were in school.

Much later in life, probably when I was in my mid-thirties, some twenty years after the incident with the gym teacher, I finally heard the rest of that story. I never knew that my eldest brother Bob, who was like a dad for me after our dad died, went to see that gym teacher when he'd heard about the boarding.

Bob was a Vietnam vet, and even though he loves the Lord now, back in those days, back in the hills, you grew up fighting if you wanted to survive. My brother Bob is still feared in Wellston, Ohio, because of the tough reputation he built when he was a much younger man.

Back in those days, he was mean as a snake and would just as soon fight you as to look at you. But he'd heard about my boarding and went to talk to that teacher. He said, "Listen to me, I know Troy is ornery. He's like all of us were when we were in school. You've known us all our lives. I get it. And if he does wrong in your class, you have my blessing to whip him with the board, and when he gets home, I'll whip him with the belt. He'll get it twice. We will not have him disrespecting you." He said his piece but wasn't quite finished with that gym teacher. He leaned in close and continued, "But let me tell you something. If you ever hit my brother that hard again, I'm going to come down here and wear you out! To break a board on a kid is over the line and I won't have it!"

But I never knew anything about that confrontation because there was no way Bob was going to uncover and undermine that man's authority in front of me. He knew that if I was aware of the conversation he'd had with my gym teacher that I'd lose respect for him and my brother Bob wanted to protect me from that.

The fact is if we want our kids to respect God's authority, we have to start teaching them to respect all the authority figures He's placed in their lives. Remember, God puts a high premium on authority, a very high premium.

Which Is the Graver Sin?

Still not convinced that God puts a premium on authority? Let me ask you an interesting question . . .

Which is the graver sin, to sin against God's holiness or against His authority?

Let me tell you a story that will reveal the answer. It's a story from the Bible of two kings, two kings with whom you are very familiar, King Saul and King David. Both of these kings sinned against God's holiness, but only one sinned against God's authority.

Remember? God told Saul, "I want you to go in and destroy the Amalekites" (1 Samuel 15). "I want you to destroy them utterly. Kill all the men, women, and children. I even want you to kill all the animals, all the sheep, goats, cows . . . everything, even their King Agag. I want you to totally destroy them."

So Saul's army goes in and attacks the Amalekites and kills everything . . . well, almost everything. He doesn't kill King Agag, and he orders his men to keep the best of the sheep alive.

God told the prophet Samuel what happened, so Samuel made the trip to see Saul and confront him about his disobedience. When confronted, Saul didn't repent; instead, he began to try to justify his sin to Samuel. He told the prophet, "Well, sure I kept some of the sheep. But they're not for me . . . I was going to sacrifice them to the Lord."

Saul tried to put his disobedience in the best possible light. If you look at it one way, Saul's not a bad guy here. He wants to donate the sheep to the church. He tells the prophet, "Look at all these fine sheep, Samuel. We're going to have a huge service, and we're going to worship and sing and sacrifice all these sheep to the Lord. We're going to have a regular camp meeting. It's going to be awesome!"

Now in today's world, Saul is a man we'd definitely keep on the church board. He may have messed up, but there's no way we're getting rid of him for that. We'd want him to continue to be our pastor, continue to lead us. We'd love him as our neighbor; he's a great guy. Today, we're totally buying into his justification of his sinful disobedience. That's consistent with today's attitude toward authority. Always submit and obey authority . . . at least as long as it seems like the right thing to do.

But now let's take a look at King David. He sleeps with Bathsheba and gets her pregnant. She's married, so he plots to have her husband murdered, signing his death warrant. So here you've got David . . . he's a lying, conniving, cheating, and adulterous murderer. How do you feel about him and what he's done compared to Saul and what he did?

Well, in today's world, you don't want anything to do with David. He's no longer welcome in church; in fact, you'd have him kicked out! You'll never have him speak from the pulpit, and you sure don't want him as your neighbor, especially if you have an attractive wife!

But let's look a little deeper. We saw Saul justifying his sinful disobedience to God's authority when confronted by the prophet Samuel. What happened when the prophet Nathan confronted David?

When Nathan stood before David to confront him, he told him a story about a greedy rich man who takes whatever he wants from whoever he wants. David is enraged and says, "Who is this man? I'll have him killed!" Nathan pointed his bony prophet's finger at David and yelled, "YOU ARE THAT MAN!" David immediately fell on his face before the Lord and cried out, "I have sinned against the Lord!" (2 Samuel 12:13).

Saul sinned against God's holiness and His authority. David sinned against God's holiness but not against God's authority. With Saul, because he didn't humble himself and repent, the Bible says, God sent an evil spirit to torment him, and he removed Saul as king.

But David was quite another matter. Even though he sinned greatly, he was quick to humble himself and repent. That's why God called David, "a man after mine own heart" (Acts 13:22). Further, because David understood God's authority, he became the king after Saul. The difference is that Saul sinned against God's authority and tried to justify it. But when David sinned against God's authority, he immediately fell on his face and repented.

How Significant Is Authority to Your Destiny?

So, let's bring this down to a personal level. How important is understanding authority in your ability to find significance?

Well, for the answer, let's look back to our story from 2 Kings about the man who lost his ax head. This man was a part of the project only because Elisha, acting under the authority of God, said, "You can go." Had Elisha turned the young man down, there would be no story in the Bible about the ax.

The fact is, if you don't recognize God's authority or worse, you recognize it but don't obey it, you'll entirely miss the purpose God has for you. And if you miss your purpose, you'll never find true significance.

This man, without the authority (Elisha) picking him, wouldn't be on that team working on that project. He wouldn't have borrowed the ax. And there would be no story about him in the Bible. It all begins with authority.

In my mind, this man's whole reason in being on the riverbank that day was to be chosen to work on that project. That way he'd have to borrow an ax and the ax head would be lost in the river, and God would perform the miracle through Elisha. God set the whole thing up because He wanted to communicate this story to us all these generations later.

Think about it—this man experienced significance when that ax head flew into the river. And the whole building project was made a part of scripture because of the miracle that occurred. And because of that, we get the benefit of reading about it and learning something about experiencing significance today.

But what if he had not recognized Elisha's authority? What if he'd been disobedient and not heeded Elisha's direction to join the team? His story wouldn't have made it into the Bible because there would have been no story to tell!

There are so many people down through history continuing to this very day who encounter God's blessing of significance in their lives because of the way they handle and understand authority.

You see this happening all through the scriptures. One example is the Roman centurion who came to Jesus with a servant at home who needed healing (Matthew 8:5-13). The man said to Jesus, "I'm a man with authority and under authority. I get it. I understand how authority works and how important it is. I know what You're about, Jesus, and I know You have authority in this situation. You don't even have to come to my house. Just speak the word, and it'll happen. All You have to do is say the word." And it did happen. Jesus spoke the word, and the centurion's servant was healed, and Jesus marveled at the man's faith.

Understanding authority is the vital first step in us being able to experience God's blessing and significance in this life. Jesus was moved by the centurion, not because of his imposing size or his impressive armor but because of his powerful faith in the authority of God. Authority puts things in order and order makes way for function, which will always lead to blessing and significance.

10

Understanding the Importance of God's Order

We talked in the last chapter about the importance of handling God's authority correctly. Authority is so critical because it's the first step in bringing things into God's divine order. You see, there is a divine order to things and it has to reign supreme in your life before you can successfully function with His blessing.

I see this as a sequence of things. First of all, **Authority** comes and puts things in their proper **Order.** Once things are in order, they can **Function** correctly. And when they function correctly, you'll be able to experience the **Blessings** that come from them.

For many years I've done my best to follow this sequence of Authority, Order, Function, and Blessing in every area of my life from the way I operate in my family to the way I serve in my church and community. I know from experience that I will never receive the blessing of any function until it comes into proper order. Further, I know that divine order will only happen once I learn how to handle and submit to the authorities that God has placed in my life.

To better illustrate what I'm talking about, think for a moment about your physical body. Your brain responds when the systems throughout your body are in order. Only then is the body able to function healthily. And when that happens, you can experience the blessing that comes from having a healthy body.

Let's say you wanted to reach up and grab a book from the top shelf at the local library. It all begins with the authority of the brain, which tells the body what it needs to do to reach that book. Because there's a proper order present in the body, the arm reaches, and maybe even the legs stretch to stand up on tiptoes. Authority and order have allowed for proper function to be able to reach that book. In this way, you can experience the blessing that comes from reaching the book on your own without having to ask for help. This sequence works the same way whether it's in your home, your church, your place of work, or in our government.

But what about when things get out of order? What do you do then? I remember a few years ago experiencing some pain in my lower back. I'm a pretty active guy and over time (and a lot of hours on the basketball court!) I had developed some nagging pain that didn't seem to go away no matter what I tried.

I was using this experience to make a point in a sermon one Sunday. After the service, one of our members, who just happened to be a chiropractor, approached me and offered to see me at no charge. He felt confident that he could help me get rid of the pain in my back.

So, I made an appointment and went in to see him. He took a few x-rays and could immediately tell precisely where my problem was. He could see where some adjustments needed to be made, and he made them. Oh, what a relief that was! No more pain! Once he made the changes and got things back into their proper alignment and order, the pain when away.

What a great picture of the importance of things being in their proper order. It doesn't matter where you might be experiencing pain, whether in your business, or your church, in your marriage, your career, or any place else, you'll never experience the blessing when things are out of their proper alignment or order.

The pain serves as a signal that something is out of order and adjustments need to be made so you can function properly and experience the blessing that comes from good health.

Ezekiel Brings Order to the Dry Bones

There's a fascinating story in Ezekiel 37 about the prophet Ezekiel and a vision that the Lord gave him. In the vision, God led Ezekiel to the middle of a valley full of old dry bones scattered all across the valley floor. The Lord directed Ezekiel to walk back and forth among the bones. Finally, the Lord asks Ezekiel, "Son of man, can these bones live?" (v. 3).

Ezekiel answered the Lord and said, "Well, you're the only One who can know that. You're the authority here." God then commanded Ezekiel to prophesy to the bones. So, Ezekiel cried out in the authority of the Word of God, "O ye dry bones, hear the word of the LORD. Thus saith the Lord GOD unto these bones; Behold, I will cause breath to enter into you, and ye shall live: And I will lay sinews upon you, and will bring up flesh upon you, and cover you with skin, and put breath in you, and ye shall live; and ye shall know that I am the LORD" (Ezekiel 37:4-6).

Once the authority of the Word of God was declared, those old dry bones that had been lying all across the floor of that dusty valley began to rattle and shake. The bones, which had been scattered, began to make their way back to where they belonged in their proper order. They came together bone to bone. Then Ezekiel saw tendons and flesh appear on the bones. Finally, the wind began to blow, and God breathed into them, and they came to life and stood up on their feet and became a giant army of soldiers.

The bones, connected according to their DNA, came into order because of the authority of the spoken Word of God. First, there were the bones, then the body, and then breath. Everything needed to be whole, healthy, and functioning. Of course, it takes all three because if you have bones without a body, you have a skeleton. If you have a body with no bones, you have a blob. If you have bones and body but no breath, you're left with a corpse. But when you have bones, body, and breath, you have a thriving, functioning army.

That's a great example of divine order instituted by the authority of God. It makes sense when we read the passage from Ezekiel. But the problem is, we make decisions every day based on things other than God's authority, and we end up missing His order. We put this bone with that bone based on any number of reasons, even though those two bones were never made to connect.

We make decisions about our significance and life purpose based on what looks right or feels right or based on other people's opinions about how things ought to be. The results rarely turn out okay.

It reminds me of the adage, "A camel is a horse designed by a committee." When decisions are being made according to personal opinions or feelings and not by the authority of God's divine order, who knows what you might end up with!

You can only find God's divine order when you're committed to following God's authority. Ezekiel spoke the prophecy (God's authority), the bones rattled and shook and came together (God's order). Then, once they were filled with the breath of Life, they were fully ready to function as God's army. This was a vision about the coming together of the nation of Israel. And the blessing of God was only able to come because all the pieces had come together in their proper place.

What Does the Sequence Have to Do with Significance?

We've learned that you don't have function until you first put things in order, which comes from God's authority. How does that translate to your life? Let's take another look at the sequence I talked about earlier. Authority leads to order, which leads to function, which finally results in the blessing of the Lord. Each thing builds on the one previous.

In an earlier chapter, we talked about that deep-down desire in all humankind to be picked for something. We all want to be chosen, and not just selected for any old thing. We want to be picked for a cause, a cause bigger than just ourselves. We know there are bigger things going on in the world and we want to be a part of them.

But the only way we're going to be available to be chosen is through God Himself. His Word, the Holy Spirit, and the authorities He's put in your life, your parents, your pastor, whoever it might be.

One of the reasons why so many never come into their purpose and destiny is because they never learn to take the first step of submitting to the authorities that God has placed in their lives. Once the proper authority is in place, order can follow. And when things are in order, you can figure out whether you are a finger or a thumb or a foot in the body of Christ. Once you know what part you are, you'll know what to do, and you'll be able to figure out your function.

Order Leads to Function

Without order, there can be no function. You can have all the parts to a car engine placed carefully under the hood of the car. But unless those parts are connected in their proper order, the car isn't going anywhere. That engine just isn't going to run. The same is true in the body of Christ.

If you spend your whole life as a Christian operating as a finger in the body of Christ but all the while you believe you should be the head, the one in charge, you're never going to function at all. You're just one thing trying to live out the function of something else entirely, and you've missed God's divine order. That's why responding to authority in your life is so important. It determines your order and function. And that's where we find purpose; it's where Life flows.

When you're cut off from authority, you can't function. Let me give you an extreme example. If I cut my hand off and lay it over in the corner of the room, it may still look like my hand, but it would never be able to function as my hand because it's not connected to my head. My head could try to command my hand to pick up a piece of fruit, but the command will never get through because there's no connection. My body can only really function when it's all connected together, and my whole body is connected to the head.

Once connected, the head can say to the hand, "Make a fist." And the hand makes a fist. This all makes sense and is obvious. But some people say, "I don't need anyone in my life telling me what to do!" And then they wonder why they're never able to get anything done. They can't function because they've cut themselves off from the authority God has placed in their lives.

The same is true when you're not operating in divine order. A foot is perfectly designed to be a foot. It's specially made to absorb the impact that the body makes on the ground as it walks or runs. It's designed perfectly. But what happens when a foot tries to ignore God's order and become an eye? All kinds of problems arise! A foot may be perfectly designed to do what it does, but it sure makes a lousy eye!

Paul addressed all this in 1 Corinthians 12:14-20, "For the body is not one member, but many. If the foot shall say, Because I am not the hand, I am not of the body; is it therefore not of the body? And if the ear shall say, Because I am not the eye, I am not of the body; is it therefore not of the body? If the whole body were an eye, where were the hearing? If the whole were hearing, where were the smelling? But now hath God set the members every one of them in the body, as it hath pleased him. And if they were all one member, where were the body? But now are they many members, yet but one body."

In that passage, when Paul says, "God set the members every one of them in the body, as it hath pleased him," he's talking about divine order. And when the body is in divine order, under the authority of the head, it can function the way it's supposed to.

Function Brings the Blessing

Now we know about authority, and we know about order and function, but what about the blessing? Where does that come in to play? Well, whether you are in the valley of dry bones or in your home on your street, when you're able to function you're able to experience the blessing of it.

In my body, my head sends the message to my leg to "KICK!" And because my leg is connected in order and under the authority of my head, my leg kicks. And I'm able to have the blessing of my leg being able to kick. Just like being able to reach the book on the top shelf of the library, I experience the blessing of being able to do that because my body is in order.

But the opposite is also true. If I've cut off my arm and lay it over in the corner of the room, there's no way it can function as my arm, and there's no way I'll be able to receive the blessing of being able to reach the book on the top shelf.

That's why this sequence is so vital when talking about significance. So many people are trying to find significance but failing to take the very first step, which is correctly handling the authorities that God has placed in their life. They may be crying out to be picked, but they will never find true significance until they submit to and respect authority.

All these are simple steps to finding significance. We want to be known but will never be chosen if we insist on our way with the desire to make our name great. If we're never chosen, we'll never get to be a part of a cause, something bigger than ourselves. We'll never be able to stand up and say, "I was here!" unless we first come under authority, find His order, operate in the proper function, and receive His blessing. Only then will we enter into our purpose, the reason for which we were born.

11

On Loan—How Can You Lose What You Do Not Own?

Did you know that you are not your own, that everything you have is on loan from God? The Bible is full of verses just like this one . . .

"What? know ye not that your body is the temple of the Holy Ghost which is in you, which ye have of God, and ye are not your own? For ye are bought with a price: therefore glorify God in your body, and in your spirit, which are God's" (1 Corinthians 6:19-20).

It's verses like these that remind us that our lives are not our own. We've been bought with a price and the life we live is on loan from God. Or to put it another way, our life is borrowed from God. Think about it, none of us were born, grew up, learned, developed, and matured all due to our own strength and will. So how did we get here? We got here because of God. He's the One who has given our lives to us. We're on loan from eternity. God is the One responsible for our lives.

God lets us borrow the breath we breathe and the strength in our bodies, and even our own unique sense of identity. And the way we repay Him is to live a life to His glory.

It's just like the story we've been following from 2 Kings 6. Our man wanted to be known, he wanted to be a part of a team, he wanted to join the cause that was bigger than him. But he didn't have any tools; he had nothing that he could bring of his own to the cause. He couldn't very well chop down trees with his bare hands! He knew that if he was going to be able to participate, he was going to have to borrow an ax. But he was willing to do whatever it took in order to join that cause. He had to borrow an ax . . . and that's typical of our life too. Our life is borrowed from God.

In fact, everything we have is borrowed from God. The possessions we may think of as ours actually belong to Him. Our finances, our house, our car, and our clothes . . . all these things were ultimately provided for us and given to us on loan by God.

When you think about it even the breath we breathe is borrowed.

Even the Breath in Our Lungs Is Borrowed

One of the most profound experiences of my life has been to witness the birth of my kids. I'm not sure that anything on this earth is as miraculous and moving as the birth of a child, especially when the child being born is yours! If anything reminds you of the reality of a holy and all-powerful God, it's childbirth.

I remember the birth of my firstborn, Katie. My wife Mandy had been up for quite a while in the night with labor pains before she decided it was finally time to wake me up and get to the hospital. Of course I was in the middle of a dead sleep and woke up startled, immediately in EMERGENCY mode. I thought that baby could come at any time and I was worried because we lived quite a distance from the closest hospital.

So here I am rushing around, trying to get Mandy and all the baby stuff into my brand-new car. I was so proud of that car! We were loading up and Mandy says to me, "Let's stop off at the store. I want to pick up a few things." Of course I wanted to get on to the hospital as soon as possible. I didn't want our baby to be born in my brand-new car along the side of the highway!

Mandy's labor pains were progressing quickly, but I made the stops she wanted me to make and we made it to the hospital just in the nick of time. In fact, Katie was born only twenty minutes after we checked in to the maternity ward.

I'll never forget the magic of that moment. Talk about being part of something bigger than you! Katie was my first child so I'm having all these "first time father" feelings. I'm crying and laughing at the same time and so proud of Mandy and so thankful to the Lord for the blessing of children. It was an emotional high for sure.

But right in the middle of all that emotion, I looked over and noticed that Katie wasn't crying. In fact, I noticed she wasn't even breathing! The doctor was holding Katie and encouraging her, "Come on, Katie. Come and join us in this world. Come to the world, Katie." But Katie wasn't taking a breath. The doctor kept on urging, "Katie, come on."

I remember standing there in shock. So much joy followed now by so much concern over what was happening with my new baby, or maybe better put, what was NOT happening with my new baby. I felt so helpless. It was probably just a few seconds but it seemed like an eternity to me. How in the world are you supposed to explain to a newborn baby how to take a breath?

The doctor's voice took on a bit more urgency when she said, "Come on, Katie. Come on, take a breath for me, Katie." Finally out of frustration I instinctively hollered out, "Just smack her!" And the doctor gave Katie a good smack on her little behind. Katie let out a gasp as she sucked in her first big gulp of this earth's air. She took her first breath and started crying. I'd never heard such a beautiful sound in all my life.

As I stood there I realized that I had been holding my own breath. I took a big gulp of air just like Katie. I watched as the doctor handed my little girl over to a crew of nurses who began to do the things nurses do with newborn babies. As they worked with little Katie, I began to think to myself, *Who told that little girl, after nine long months in her mother's womb, how to breathe?* The doctor was powerless to make her breathe. I was powerless to make her breathe. Her mother was powerless to make her breathe. There wasn't a thing I could do to make my little Katie take that first breath. But . . . God simply said, "Breathe, Katie, I want to give you breath."

God is the One who loaned her that first breath, and He's been loaning breaths to her ever since. Just like He does with me and with you and with everyone who's ever been born into this world. We're powerless on our own. The truth is, without God we can't even take a breath. All of us are on loan from God.

We own nothing.

We don't even own the breath in our nostrils. If you don't believe me just sit beside a loved one who is dying, struggling to take the next breath. If it were in our power to bring breath to a loved one, we'd do it in a heartbeat. But the fact is we're powerless. No matter what we may try to do, we can't take the air and force it into someone's lungs causing them to breathe.

God gives us the lungs in our bodies. He gives us the capacity to take in air . . . the ability to breathe. Even the air we breathe belongs to Him. So here's what I'm wondering . . . if we don't even own the air we breathe in and breathe out, just over 23,000 times a day every day, what makes us think we own the house we live in or the car that we drive? What makes us think we own the money in our pocket or the clothes on our backs? We own nothing that God hasn't blessed us with. He is responsible for it all.

How Can You Lose What's Not Yours?

Years ago, I began to feel that God was telling me it was time to move our church. I was aware of an empty car dealership not far from our location. I had even purchased a car from that dealership when it was open. The building was perfectly located right off one of the major highway loops around our city. It was an ideal location for us, visible from the road, easily accessible from anywhere in town. And yet I was reluctant to pursue the move. Moving is always a daunting task, much more so in this situation. I wasn't just considering moving my family. I was thinking about the enormous effort involved in moving the entire church. The task seemed like it might be more than I was prepared to mess with.

I mean, I'll admit, I was pretty comfortable right where I was. Why mess with a good thing? I wasn't an old man by any stretch and still had many years of productive ministry out in front of me. I had a beautiful wife and four kids. I felt like I had arrived in a good place. And yet, I couldn't shake the nagging sense that God was calling us to move our church into that abandoned car dealership.

I argued back and forth with God for months. I reasoned with God, explaining to Him (as if He needed me to!) that we already had a beautiful campus on fifty acres with a nice building, doing three morning services every Sunday. There were three or four other buildings on the property so we had options for growth in the future if we wanted to. We didn't have much debt and had a nice lump of cash in the bank. I felt I could serve there for the rest of my life, making no changes at all. We were drawing a decent crowd every weekend; I was making a good salary. I was comfortable. I had it all, certainly compared to many who serve in ministry.

I argued with God, "Why in the world would I want to move?" For two years I fought with God and in all that time, the dealership never sold. Others had tried to buy it and do something with it but every attempt fell through and the building continued to sit empty. I had to pass right by that place most days and every time I looked over it was like a punch in the gut.

Finally one day, I pulled in to the parking lot and took a look around. I called one of the elders of the church and told him about the whole idea of moving to the dealership. I asked him, "Does that just sound crazy to you?" He said, "Well, I don't know if it sounds crazy or not. You never know. It might just be the Lord."

So I continued to toss the idea around for a few more days, praying about it. I called the property owners and they said there were five other groups interested in the place, there were a couple of churches and some other businesses. I listened as they told me their terms. They wanted a million dollars in cash up front and then we could just assume their current lease.

I tossed and turned in bed that night and struggled to fall asleep. I prayed to the Lord and said, "God, You know I'm not one for 'putting out a fleece.' I've always tried to be led by Your Holy Spirit. But if You want me to even think about doing this, I'm asking You to remove that million dollar down payment from the equation and everybody else interested in that property needs to drop out." In my mind, that had settled the matter. I rolled over and went to sleep.

The next day I met the owner and asked him if he would show me the building. We arrived in the parking lot and got out of the car but before he showed me anything he said, "I just need to tell you something. The owners met last night. It was crazy. For three years now, there have been lots of people trying to buy this property to do something with it and everything has fallen through. We've recently had five people coming to us with offers. But as of last night, all five of them have dropped out. They're no longer interested. So we decided we would drop the requirement of the million dollar down payment if you'll just assume the lease."

You could have picked me up off the pavement of that parking lot! Clearly, the Lord had answered my prayer but that's when I got really nervous because now I knew I was going to have to be obedient. I met with our elders and things progressed pretty quickly after that. Not only did we take possession of the dealership, we were able to sell our old church and property. God took over and the whole deal happened in a couple of weeks.

Throughout that whole process I stewed over and over with the "what ifs." What if the deal falls through? What if there are unforeseen issues with the new place and it ends up being a money pit? What if we can't sell our old building? What if we end up without a building at all? What if we lose everything . . . What if . . . .

And just so sweetly and gently, God slipped His loving arm around me and said, "Well, that's interesting, son." And I said, "What's that, Lord?" He said, "Well, how can you lose what's not yours in the first place? I didn't know any of this was yours. Not your church, not your building, not your congregation. So you're telling Me that you're afraid you're going to lose something? Let Me remind you that you can't lose something you don't have to begin with."

The Lord continued to speak, "You see, son, everything in this life is just like the manna in the wilderness. The moment you try to take hold of something that doesn't belong to you, it's going to go bad." He continued, "It's all mine. Your life, your breath, this church, that car, your family, everything you have is borrowed. It all belongs to Me."

He let me "borrow an ax" to swing so I could join His cause. But I learned the lesson that the ax very clearly belongs to Him. I said to Him that day, "From now on, I'll do whatever You want me to do, Lord. I'll swing the ax You told me to swing."

Nothing belongs to us, including our breath. It's all a borrowed ax.

12

Significance Through Surrender

Have you ever noticed the interesting thing we ask when we're first introduced to someone? When we're in a place where we're meeting someone new, what's the first question we're likely to ask them? We don't ask them what kind of car they drive or what their favorite football team is, at least not at first. Of all the things we could ask to get to know them better, we normally lead off with, "What do you do?"

Isn't that interesting that the qualifier we normally choose in which to get to know someone better is to ask what they do, what is their job. We want to know what it is that they've been able to accomplish in their life. At some level, we believe this will be the best indicator of what kind of person they are.

And even though we might like to think otherwise, we're all guilty of judging someone very differently according to how they answer that question. I know you know what I'm talking about! If they say, "I dig ditches," you're going to think one thing about them. But if they say, "I'm the CEO of a multi-million dollar corporation," you're going to evaluate them very differently.

In our culture today, all of us tend to place much more value on someone's accomplishments than on the person they are. And because we all know that's true, we tend to measure ourselves in the same way. We compare ourself with our neighbor or the person sitting next to us in the office or at church. We strive for significance by earning more, owning more, and doing more, while many times ignoring the challenge to BE MORE.

Believe me, I get it. We tend to strive for significance by measuring ourselves with others by comparing the things we own. And now here I am telling you in the last chapter that we own nothing! It's all on loan from God! So let me dive a little deeper into that subject to explain what I mean.

We've been studying the man in 2 Kings 6 and his search for significance. He started by saying, "Hey, pick me! I want to be a part of a cause, a cause bigger than me. You don't even have to know my name. I want to join the cause so much, I'm even willing to humble myself and borrow an ax so I'll have a tool to work with."

When we can come to an understanding, like the man in 2 Kings, that we own nothing in this life, it makes it much easier for us to surrender ourselves to Him. Once we're able to grasp the fact that it all belongs to the Lord in the first place, we can stop struggling and striving for more. We can finally step off the treadmill of striving and yearning for things like status and position.

In my own life, I came to the place where God was finally able to get that message through to me. I finally got it. Today I'm very clear on the fact that I don't own anything. I'm merely a steward of what God has loaned me. Even the very breath I breathe is on loan from Him.

Once I got that, it was much easier for me to understand His authority. And once I understood that everything comes from Him, I was able to submit to His authority in my life. I was able to say, "Lord, I'm here and I can swing whatever ax You tell me to swing." My significance isn't going to be about the things I own because I don't own anything. I can really only find true significance when I understand that reality.

That's why I love the story from 2 Kings 6. Lots of folks hear that story and believe that the main message is the miracle that Elisha performed. Elisha prayed and the ax head rose to the surface of the water. Many people just accept that that is the primary lesson to be gained from that story. And don't get me wrong, that's a great lesson, making for a great story.

But I believe the real crux of that story lies a little deeper. I believe the main message is that the ax that the man was using was borrowed from someone else! The man had nothing with which to bring to the table. Even the ax he was using to cut down trees had to be borrowed from another student.

You see, just like that man, we wouldn't be a part of a cause or anything else if God didn't lend us the resources, the ability, the breath. I mean, in my case, how in the world am I going to even be able to preach without first being able to breathe? I could be the most gifted preacher in the country but unless God first gives me breath, I'm unable to utter a single word.

The Rest of the Story

In the last chapter I told you the story about God leading us to move our church from a very nice, comfortable place on fifty acres to another location in an old car dealership. Let me give you a little peek into the back story . . .

In the story, I told you that I spent months wrestling with God about making that move. But what I didn't tell you was that God had been talking to me for some time about trimming back the ministry of the church a bit. I really felt that God was leading me to get the church lean for some reason. Of course, now I know He was preparing us for the move but at the time, I didn't know that. I just thought He was asking me to pare back and trim down.

Now you have to understand, I'm a "big picture" thinker, I'm a dreamer. I like to "go big or go home." Many times I believe that the bigger my dreams are the better they are. So the last thing I wanted to hear from anyone is that I need to cut out, trim down, or prune back.

One week it all seemed to come to a head. I was in prayer about the upcoming weekend service and God confronted me with the question, "Are you going to do what I'm telling you to do?" I said, "What do You mean, Lord?" He said, "I want you to get up in front of the congregation and tell them what we've been talking about, that it's time to trim back." I argued back with Him, "I haven't even talked to the elders about that yet!" He said, "That's your own fault. I've been dealing with you on this for a long while. You go up there and tell the congregation."

I knew I needed to be obedient but I was still struggling with it. I was stuck with the desire to grow and get bigger, not cut back and trim down. Then the Lord said, "I've got one last question for you." I said, "What is it, Lord?" That's when He played His trump card. He simply said, "Would you like to preach by yourself on Sunday or would you like for Me to do it with you?"

He had me. I said, "I have to have You with me, Lord. I don't want to go without You." He said, "You go up there and tell them what's going to happen." In that moment, I realized that He is the ultimate authority in my life and that without Him, I am nothing. I knew that everything I own and everything I am, even my ability to preach, comes from Him and Him alone.

The Peace You Find Through Surrender

The problem, of course, is that many people are afraid that if they let go of their tight hold of ownership on their lives that they'll lose everything they've worked so hard for. But the opposite is true. Letting go actually brings with it a wave of peace and an inward sense of knowing that it's all going to be okay.

Make no mistake, I know, letting go is a tough thing to do. Just thinking about surrendering everything can cause fear to come and drape itself across your shoulders like a heavy wet blanket. In fact, psychologists will tell you that the fear of loss is one of the biggest motivators there is. The fear that you'll lose everything you've worked so hard for . . . all gone.

It's this powerful attack of fear that causes so many to grasp and clutch to get and keep everything they can. They figure if they don't hold on tight to everything that they'll lose it all and if they lose it all, they'll also lose whatever significance they've built up along the way.

That's why this message of surrender is so freeing. Surrendering it all to God doesn't mean He takes it away. It just means you realize that everything you thought you possessed, including your gifts and talents, is on loan from Him.

Let me ask you . . . who would you be and what would you do if there was no fear of failing or losing? Let me put it another way: what opportunities have you passed up because you were afraid that if you tried, you might fail? What dreams have you discounted because you were afraid that the dream was too big, too much for you to accomplish?

Fear can be such an imposing enemy for all of us. It keeps even the best of us, the strongest of us, cowering and unwilling to pursue even the godly dreams He places in our hearts. So many hold back and don't even try things because of the fear of failure and loss.

But here's the freeing part of what I'm trying to get across to you. Be encouraged with this, you cannot fail when the dream isn't yours to begin with. You can't fail when you don't have anything to lose! When you understand that everything belongs to God anyway, it frees you up to go for it!

Dear friend, what could you accomplish for His Kingdom if you knew you wouldn't fail, you *couldn't* fail? People put incredible pressure on themselves because they believe that their significance is tied to their success and it's unthinkable to imagine failure. They slip so easily from "It failed" to "I'm a failure." Understanding that you can't fail because it's all on loan from Him in the first place is an incredibly freeing thing.

Of course, this understanding keeps you humble, helping you deal with pride and greed. If you know that it all comes from God, you have nothing to be haughty about!

Your significance doesn't come from what you own or from what you've been able to accomplish or accumulate in life. Your significance comes from God. Your significance is borrowed from Him.

It All Goes Back in the Box

So many spend a lifetime caught up in the rat race of accumulating things. They just don't understand that God puts much more emphasis on who you are rather than what you have. As we all know, nothing you accumulate here on this earth will go with you when you die.

I once heard a story about a man playing the game of Monopoly with his family. He loved playing this game, and he was good at it. Over the course of the game, he accumulated more money and more property than anyone else. He was relishing in the fact that he was winning. He had cash on the table, stashed in his pockets, and even up his sleeves. And every time someone else landed on one of his properties, he got even more cash. He was really a terrible winner, gloating in his sure victory.

One by one, each of his family members dropped out of the game. It just wasn't fun for them anymore. This guy was making the game miserable for everyone else. It was late and his family wandered off to bed and he was left alone to pick up the game all by himself.

He was bragging to himself, imagining how successful he was. Even though it was just a game, he was brimming with significance and self-importance. He'd obviously won the game but he couldn't help counting his money and adding up the value of all the property he'd accumulated. He carefully sorted the cash and put it all back in the box along with the property deeds, the dice, the cards, and finally the little thimble, the old shoe, the top hat, and even the little Scotty dog. It all went back in the box.

It was in that quiet moment that God spoke to the man. He said, "Son, this game is much more like life than you can imagine." "How so, Lord?" the man asked. "You live your life striving for things like money and property and buildings. You imagine that these things are so important and so critical to winning, to your success and significance. But in the end, when it's all over, it all goes back in the box. All that striving and all that effort but when it's all said and done, it all goes back in the box. You don't take anything with you when it's over."

In that moment the man understood. Life is not about property and houses and hotels and cash. Those things are all on loan from God. If we have any of those things in this life, they are only borrowed from Him and when we die, it all goes back in the box.

Like the old adage, "You never see an armored car following a hearse to the graveyard!" We all know that you can't take it with you, but we don't live our lives that way. We live as if this life is all about accumulating things that we can take with us into eternity. And in some way we believe that our "rank" in eternity is determined by what we are able to accomplish in this life.

But that's a lie! Our significance in this life isn't determined by what we have or what we do. Our significance is based on who we are. And who are we? We are God's children, His sons and daughters. Our identity is found in Him . . . it's borrowed from Him! Colossians 3:3 says very clearly, "For ye are dead, and your life is hid with Christ in God." Our lives are "hid with Christ." Our identity, our significance isn't found in what we own; it's found in who owns us! We are found in Him!

Let me ask you . . . why are you holding back from going for the dreams that God has placed in your heart? Are you fearful that you'll try and fail? Are you afraid if you surrender everything you have to Him that you'll end up losing it all? My friend, now is not the time to grab and clutch; it's time to let go and surrender it all to Him. It's His anyway! Let's go for it. Let's be everything God has asked us to be.

In my case, once I understood that my significance is only found in complete surrender to Him, then whether He wants me to leave my church and go up in the hills to some little country church and minister to a little congregation of about twenty people or go into the big city and pastor a church of thousands, it doesn't matter! I've surrendered to Him! It all belongs to Him!

There was a time when surrender was much easier for me. When I first started out in ministry I didn't have a thing. I had no wife or kids to be responsible for. When I first started preaching and pastoring it was just me.

I thought, *Well, this surrendering stuff is pretty easy!* I had no money, nothing in the bank. I came out of the hills with literally nothing. If God had asked me to go to the deepest darkest jungle and share the Gospel with the people there, it would have been easy to do. I had nothing to lose. Let me tell you, surrender is pretty easy when you have nothing to lay on the line.

But these days, surrender is tougher for me and as you accumulate more and become more successful, it will be tougher for you too. You've worked hard and now you've got a little bit of retirement saved up. You're living in a nice warm house with some money in the bank. Maybe you're driving a new car, able to take bigger and better vacations. Now God says, "I want you to put it all on the line with the risk of losing every bit of it."

This is when surrender gets tough. We reach a certain place in life where surrendering becomes much more difficult to do. No matter what arena of life you're talking about, business, education, government, or ministry, the more you accumulate the tougher it's going to be to surrender.

But when you realize that all you have is borrowed from Him, it's much easier to surrender to Him and what He wants you to do with your life. It's only then that you'll truly find significance, when you surrender to Him.

What Will You Do with Your Borrowed Ax?

In Matthew 25 (verses 14-30) Jesus tells the parable of the talents. It's a powerful story about a man who had three servants. Before going on a long journey he gave one servant five talents, to another he gave two talents, and to the last servant, he gave one talent.

When the master returned home from his journey he found that the first two servants had invested their talents and doubled the master's money. But the third servant was fearful and scared that he'd lose the talent so he buried it in the ground. He proudly turned it back into the master telling him, "See, you have what is yours."

That servant had missed the point entirely and was severely punished! The master wanted to see his servants invest those talents! He wanted to see what his servants would do with his money. I believe that even if they'd lost the money he wouldn't have punished them. The one who was punished was the one who was too fearful to even try. He squandered the opportunity that the master had given him and was judged harshly because of it.

We've each been given talents on loan from God. He wants to see how we are going to invest them. What are you going to do with your borrowed ax? It's not the time to be fearful and bury your talents and dreams in the ground. It's time to go for it! I'll ask again, "What would you do if you knew you couldn't fail?" That opens up a wealth of possibilities, doesn't it?

Please don't equate surrender with a negative connotation of giving up and losing out. Sure, submitting to the Lord and recognizing that you don't really own anything at all . . . that it all belongs to God, can seem like a negative message, especially if you've worked hard to fill your life with things.

It's only natural to feel a strong sense of accomplishment for all you've been able to accumulate and to resist the message that it doesn't really belong to you anyway. Believe me, I get that.

But I want you to understand my passion about this. This message isn't a negative one, it's POSITIVE! And not only positive, once you are really able to grasp the essence of what I'm trying to say, you'll find it so freeing! It takes away all the stress and oppression just to know that you are a steward and not an owner.

Now you have the freedom to really go for it. Dear reader, it's time to dream again. And it's time to pursue those dreams with no fear of failure. When you finally surrender to Him what is His anyway, you'll find the significance you are seeking so desperately!

13

The Wiggly Ax Head— What to Do When Life Breaks

In our story about the man with the borrowed ax from 2 Kings 6, the man is searching for significance. He wants to be a part of a cause that's bigger than himself, so he borrows an ax and crosses the river and begins to work on the building project by cutting down trees.

But his ax is borrowed and the ax head is a little wiggly on the handle. Suddenly, at the height of one of his mighty backswings, the ax head flies off the ax handle and lands in the middle of the river, sinking quickly to the muddy bottom.

This is where the whole story turns. Things are looking good. He's borrowed an ax, and he's hard at work on the project. He's feeling right about being a part. He's contributing, he's helping, he feels like maybe he's finally arrived. And then . . .

. . . his borrowed ax breaks.

The same thing happens to us. We're all born with a wiggly ax head and often don't even realize it. Life seems to be going along okay. Sure, maybe it's not what you thought it would be, but it's not too bad. You've grown up and made it through school, you've got a family, a good job. You're part of something good, and you're swinging your ax. You're contributing; you're in the groove and doing your best.

But at some point, life breaks and all of a sudden your story pivots, just like the man in 2 Kings 6. You start by wanting to be known . . . your soul cries out, "I am here!" You're fine even if no one knows your name. You raise your hand and say, "Hey, pick me!" You want to join the cause, you want to be part of something bigger than you . . . but you will never truly grasp the significance of these steps until your wiggly ax head breaks.

You may have grown up in a Christian home, never missing a chance to go to church. Maybe you've read through the Bible dozens of times and have memorized hundreds of verses. But you'll never really be able to grasp the concept of grace until you come face to face with the reality that your ax head has come off, your life is broken, and you need a Savior.

I can promise you that, at some point, your life is going to break. I've said before, there are two kinds of people in this world, broken people and people who will become broken; it's only a matter of time.

It happens to everybody. You can be swinging along doing great, cutting down trees, when suddenly your ax head flies off the handle and you're standing there with only an ax handle in your hands, no longer able to cut down trees, no longer able to be effective, no longer part of a cause. You're standing there with your life shattered in pieces around your ankles.

Maybe your spouse comes in from work one day and wants a divorce. Or perhaps you get a bad diagnosis from the doctor that you didn't see coming. Maybe you encounter a significant failure of some kind, and your life crashes around you. Maybe life crumbles because of just one bad decision. It could be anything, but all of us, at some point, are going to have to deal with a broken life. Everything was going along just fine, but then, all of a sudden, your ax head flies off into the water.

It happened suddenly, entirely unanticipated. It seemed like everything was going along just fine. Now you're muttering to yourself, "I never dreamed . . ." or "At thirty years old, I never imagined I'd be here." Or, "I just never thought this would happen to me. I didn't expect that I'd ever do that. I never imagined I'd be capable of such a thing."

Sound familiar? We've all been there. And if you haven't been there yet, let me be the first to break the news, it's coming. Believe me, in my years of ministry I've heard these phrases dozens of times from people who end up in my office, head in their hands, saying these things to themselves as much as they're saying these things to me. Rest assured, my friend, every single person who has lived in this world has had their ax break. Everyone's life breaks at some point.

When My Wiggly Ax Head Broke

You may be asking yourself, "I wonder if Troy has ever had to deal with a broken ax?" Well, I'd love to tell you that my life has been a breeze, just living from blessing to blessing! But like I said, everyone's life will break at some point. And mine did too.

I was a young pastor, only twenty-five years old. I was serving at a great church, one that was encountering unprecedented growth. I was riding a wave of success and blessing like I'd never experienced before in my life.

And then the ax broke.

I made some poor choices and the resulting circumstances brought me to the lowest place I'd ever been. I went from feeling like I was on top of the world to feeling like I was just like that broken ax head, lying in the muddy depths of that murky river. I was hurt, confused, frustrated, emotionally drained and full of insecurity. My confidence was at an all-time low. No matter what I tried, I knew this was something I could not fix.

I knew I was done in the ministry so I immediately resigned from my position and stepped down. My career in ministry was over. I had crossed the line; I'd done too much. Now I was done.

There I was . . . a young pastor of a growing church. We'd gone from thirty people when I came to the church as a twenty-three-year-old, and the church exploded. In just a few years, we were able to buy a building with a

2,500 seat sanctuary. I was widely recognized for my preaching ability and had my pick of all the great guest preaching opportunities. I was preaching at all the camp meetings. Everything was going my way.

Now my life looked as if someone had tossed a hand grenade into it. I was at the lowest point in my life. I was disgraced and had stepped away from my position at the church. I felt like I'd been hit by a freight car, my life had been turned upside down. I was down and out and going crazy. I couldn't figure out what had happened in my life.

I publicly confessed to the church and handed in my minister's license. I resigned and walked away from ministry once and for all. I was prepared to pursue something else altogether with my life. Where I come from, when you've failed in some way, you have no chance to preach again. You're done.

But along came Don Pfeifer. You remember Don Pfeifer. I told you all about him earlier in the book. He's the preacher who called me down front and talked to me as a little ten-year-old boy at a country revival about the gift of preaching. He's the reason I wanted to be a preacher when I grew up. I looked up to him so much ever since that revival and had always viewed him as a pastor and a mentor in my life. The minute he heard about my situation (news like this always travels fast!) he called me on the telephone.

Together with a couple of other men I respected and admired they gathered around me and said, "You're not done. You're not done at all." They pulled me in and embraced me and led me through counseling and healing.

I thought I was finished with the ministry. I assumed I'd have to do something else. But Don looked at me and said, "Troy, you're an incredibly gifted preacher. Everybody has problems." He said, "Believe me, I've been at this for quite a few years, and I've walked through situations just like this with other guys. Listen to me. You are not done. It's just the beginning for you." He continued, "And one more thing, I know you're not done yet because you're the one who's supposed to take over my church when I retire!"

That encounter completely changed the course of my life. I was still a young man but had already been through almost ten years of life in ministry. Now, at thirty years of age, I felt like I was starting all over, and in many ways, I was. I went through an intense time of healing and counseling, with the local church surrounding me with love and care. In the end, Don was right. I took over his church for him when he was ready to step down.

Listen, I know firsthand, everybody's redeemable. I don't care what you've done, what you've said, what kind of life you've lived, or how bad your life was broken, YOU ARE NOT DONE! You're not nearly done. God still has a plan.

I've experienced this firsthand. I thought I was done. I had hit the absolute bottom. I had nowhere else to turn. I had lost everything. I lost my good name and my reputation. In many ways, I was that ax head. My life had been flung off the handle, and now I was that piece of iron lying in the mud in the river bottom. I know exactly what you're going through because I've been there and done that. I've lived it and come through on the other side.

What to Do When Life Breaks—The Three Options

In my years of ministry, I've counseled with hundreds of people who have had to travel the arduous journey of a broken life. I've seen shattered lives, devastation, and destruction, some because of poor choices, some just because we all live in a fallen world and life breaks. But in my experience, I can tell you that when someone's life breaks, they respond in one of three ways.

Option 1: In this option, when life breaks, some people continue to go through the motions. Their ax breaks and they go on as if nothing has happened. Like the man from 2 Kings 6, he's working with probably a hundred other guys all working hard on the project. Our man loses his ax head and, plunk, it lands in the middle of the river. But in this option, he does a very strange thing. He continues to swing his ax handle, hitting the bottom of the tree. He's not chopping anything, but he pretends that everything is okay.

Most people spend their lives just swinging an ax handle with no ax head, going through the motions, pretending everything is just fine, even though their life is going to hell, literally. People call out, "How's it going?" "Oh, it's going well. Can't complain. 'Bout as good as can be expected."

When all the while, things are falling apart at home. Things are falling apart at work. Things are falling apart emotionally, financially, and spiritually. "How are you doing with the Lord?" "Oh, everything's going great." They still come to church, and they pretend that all is well, but they're just going through the motions; their ax head is lying at the bottom of the river, and they're swinging an ax handle with no ax head.

How many times have you got up and put on your Sunday clothes, plaster a smile across your face and do your best to act like everything's okay when you're actually living in the midst of destruction? You're swinging the ax but not cutting down any trees.

Option 2: In option two, you tell yourself that you can fix the problem all by yourself. You think you don't need anybody. Sure, you recognize that there's a problem, but you don't ask for help. Instead, you prefer to try to fix things on your own. You lose the ax head in the water and instead of asking for help you rush down to the water and jump in and start looking for the ax head. You say, "I've got this. I'll fix it myself."

The man in the story could've rushed down and jumped in the river and looked for the ax head all on his own. But maybe the water was deep, and the deeper it gets, the darker it gets. And sometimes there are dangerous currents down deep that can quickly pull you under.

He goes down underwater and feels around in the mud, but he can't stay under for long. He needs to take a breath. So he comes back up, but now the current has carried him downstream. He's lost his place and no longer remembers exactly where the ax head went into the water. He goes back under, but this time he can't fight the current and is unable to even get to the bottom. He fights and fights but is losing his strength quickly. Soon he goes under and never comes back up.

In my years of ministry I've seen hundreds of people drowning in a life that's broken, trying to fix something they cannot fix. They work until they're exhausted spending money they don't have, traveling to the ends of the earth, talking until they're blue in the face, but it's all just swinging an empty ax handle. They're hitting that tree, but they're unable to cut it down.

When life breaks, most people do one of these two things. They ignore it and keep swinging, or they say, "I've got this. I can fix it on my own."

The reality is, life is going to break. It happens to us all. In fact, God will often allow our life to break in order to get our attention. You see, it's only when our life breaks that we can really experience His grace, His mercy, and His power in our lives.

The apostle Paul said it like this, "And he (God) said unto me, My grace is sufficient for thee: for my strength is made perfect in weakness. Most gladly therefore will I rather glory in my infirmities, that the power of Christ may rest upon me. Therefore I take pleasure in infirmities, in reproaches, in necessities, in persecutions, in distresses for Christ's sake: for when I am weak, then am I strong" (2 Corinthians 12:9-10).

Option 3: So, if ignoring the problem is Option 1 and insisting on trying to fix the problem on your own is Option 2, what's the third option? The third option is to cry out to the Lord for help immediately!

The man in our story immediately recognized the broken ax and cried out for help. He knew that without an ax head he had no chance of being an effective tree cutter. He knew he'd never be successful chopping down trees.

In my imagination, I see the man, watching that ax head fly into the river and in an instant he sees his future life flash before his eyes. He thinks, "I'm going to accomplish nothing with my life. I could spend all my days swinging this ax handle and cut nothing down at all. Significance? I'm crazy now to even hope for that. There's no way. I'll have absolutely no effect on this project now. I won't be able to walk by the finished building and tell others that I cut even one tree down. I thought I would be able to say to my children one day, 'See that log right there at the side of the building? That's the one I cut.' But now I won't have any of that. I will live out my life having cut nothing."

All this flashes through his mind in an instant. Instinctively he turns around and cries out to the prophet. Second Kings 6:5 says, " . . . and he cried, and said, Alas, master! for it was borrowed."

It's like he was crying out to the prophet, "Help! This is out of my control." In the story, the prophet Elisha represents the Word of God. He's God's man. When he speaks, it's like us picking up the Bible. So when this man turns to Elisha, he's turning to God.

He says, "God, this is so hard. What am I going to do now? I wasn't able to work because I had no ax. So I found this one to borrow. It had a wiggly ax head, but I was glad to get it. And now, it's broken and every breath I take, it hurts. I recognize that even the breath I breathe is borrowed, but every time I take a breath, it hurts. What am I going to do? Help me!"

Believe me, I know what it feels like in this pit of despair. I know what it's like to see everything you've worked for just circling the drain. It's all over. There's nothing redeemable. Maybe you've worked hard for a job and gotten it but now it's been taken away. You're done. Perhaps you have been guilty of making some bad choices, and now you feel that your life is broken and you're swinging an ax handle with no ax head. Your effectiveness is gone — no chance of success, no opportunity for significance.

Remember what Paul wrote in the verses I mentioned earlier? "Therefore I take pleasure in infirmities, in reproaches, in necessities, in persecutions, in distresses for Christ's sake: for when I am weak, then am I strong" (2 Corinthians 12:10).

When we are at our weakest, that's when God is at His strongest. No matter what has happened in your life, no matter how badly your life has been broken, God is standing right by your side, just waiting for you to cry out to Him for help. You can't ignore the problem, and you cannot fix it on your own. In your moment of greatest need, that's when He rushes to your side with a miracle on His mind.

14

The Stick— God's Solution for Your Brokenness

The Third Option: Cry Out to the Lord!

In the last chapter we talked about what people tend to do when faced with a broken ax . . . a broken life. We said they usually pick one of three different choices. They either ignore the brokenness entirely, continuing on as if nothing had happened. Or they will recognize the brokenness but they don't ask for help. They insist on trying to fix things, things which they can never fix on their own.

But there's a third option and that is the one I want to center in on in this chapter. What did our man from 2 Kings 6 do when he realized his ax was broken? He immediately cried out for help. Remember 2 Kings 6:5? " . . . and he cried, and said, Alas, master! for it was borrowed."

The third option is to immediately recognize the brokenness and cry out to God for help! Brother and sister, we're all broken. We've all messed up at some point in our lives. The only option when we come to the end of ourselves is to cry out to God. In that moment of crisis and brokenness, all humanity turns to God and says, "My life is borrowed and now it's broke and I can't fix it . . . I don't know what to do! Lord, help me!"

Remember the woman in the New Testament who had suffered for years with a terrible hemorrhage? She'd spent all her savings on doctors who only took her money and offered her no solutions. So what did she do? What did her desperation drive her to? She struggled to make her way through the crowd and reached out to Jesus and found her miracle (Luke 8:43-48).

Even the prodigal son (from Luke 15), as foolish as he was, knew what to do when he had "come to himself." He said, "I will arise and go to my father" (v. 18). He immediately stopped what he was doing and went home to his father.

What did Peter do when he was walking on the water and began to sink? He immediately "cried, saying, 'Lord, save me'" (see Matthew 14:30). What about Jonah? Or Moses? Or the apostle Paul? Examples are all through scripture. What do you do when your life breaks? You cry out to the only One who can save you. You cry out to the Lord.

God Cuts Down a Stick

So when our life breaks, what do we do? We cry out to the Lord to help. And what does He do when He hears our cry? Let's look again at 2 Kings 6 to see what Elisha did when confronted with that problem. When the man cried out, Elisha asks where the ax head went into the water and the man told him. The Bible says that Elisa "cut down a stick" and threw it in the river . . . toward the problem.

God does the very same thing when your life breaks and you cry out to Him. He cuts down a stick, which is the Cross of Christ. And then He puts the cross right into the middle of your situation. The stick is the cross! God cut a stick and He threw it from heaven. When Jesus hung on the cross, He was between two thieves and between two worlds. He was God's answer for humanity's brokenness. When Elisha threw the stick in the water, the Bible says the ax head began to float. The stick in the water drew out God's miracle for mankind like a poultice draws poison out of a wound.

Like we talked about in the last chapter, everybody will have their own unique "when it breaks" experience. It'll look different for every person but you can rest assured, we'll all have our own unique encounter with brokenness at some point in our life. You can ignore it, you can try to fix the problem on your own, but neither of those options will get you the solution you desire or the miracle you need. It's only when we cry out to God that we find the answers to our problems.

God's answer to our brokenness is . . . the stick! The man with the broken ax turned to Elisha and he cut a stick. We turn to God and He cuts a stick. His stick is the cross. His answer was to send His Son into our world and mend our brokenness.

Jesus Christ, and Him Crucified!

God cut a stick from eternity and sent His Son Jesus Christ, whose sole purpose in coming to earth was to go to the cross and die for the sake of humanity and our brokenness. The whole of the Bible centers on the Cross of Christ. Our lives are the same way. They hinge on the cross. When we accept what Christ did on the cross, we find the solution to our broken life. The cross is everything!

In our story, the whole thing hinges on that stick. The story is basically told in two parts, the part before the stick and what happens after the stick is thrown into the river. It's the same with each of us. Our lives are in two distinct parts, the first part, before the cross and the next part, our lives once we've recognized the cross. Everything hinges on the Cross of Christ!

That's why the apostle Paul said this, "For I determined not to know any thing among you, save Jesus Christ, and him crucified" (1 Corinthians 2:2). He said, "I'm not even going to talk about anything else. Nothing is as important as the cross!" That's the stick!

Think about it . . . the Gospel is all about Christ. It's His story, His life, His death, His burial, and His resurrection. The Gospel is about all those things. And Paul said, "For I am not ashamed of the gospel of Christ: for it is the power of God unto salvation to everyone that believeth" (Romans 1:16).

Notice here what Paul doesn't say. He doesn't say that the Gospel of Christ "has power." No. He said it IS the power! The Gospel of Christ is the full demonstration of God's power in this earth. Opening blind eyes or unstuffing deaf ears or causing the dumb to talk or the lame to walk or even raising the dead are all amazing miracles to be sure.

But none of those things make up the *full* demonstration of God's power. That distinction is reserved for Jesus Christ and Him crucified. The fullness of God's power is represented in the Cross of Christ. Only the cross can draw our significance out of the painful brokenness that we've each hidden down deep in our soul and cause it to swim to the surface so we can grab on to it, deal with it, and find healing.

The Stick Is a Magnet

Imagine dropping your favorite ink pen down in the crack between the driver's seat and the center console in your car. You try reaching it with your hand from every angle possible to no avail. You position the seat all the way up and try with no luck. You push the seat all the way back but you're still unable to reach the pen. It's so frustrating. You can look down in the crack and see your pen as plain as day. It's right there, just beyond your reach.

You're about ready to give up when you remember the magnet you keep in the junk drawer in the kitchen. (I think just about everyone has a drawer like that somewhere in their house. It's full of tape, string, wire, a few nails, some glue, and . . . a magnet!) You get the magnet and a length of string and head back to the driveway where you tie the string onto the magnet and lower it down in the crack.

All you have to do is make a single pass and the powerful pull from the magnet attracts the pen and SNAP, the pen is drawn up and out of its hiding place and sticks to the magnet. Now all you have to do is pull your pen out. Just like that!

The same is true with the Cross of Christ. When you allow God to pass the cross over the murky waters of your life, the brokenness, the sin, the hurt and pain, the bitterness and disappointment, whatever it is that has caused your life to break rises to the surface. It comes up to where you can grab onto it and deal with it once and for all.

God Brings Us All to Brokenness

Many may not want to hear this but I believe it is key. God brings us all to this critical point of brokenness. Why? Does He do it because He likes to see us in pain? NO! He does it because He knows that when our life breaks, we'll cry out for Him.

It may seem counter-intuitive but brokenness is a necessary part of growth. Before a seed can bring forth new life, it first has to die; it has to be broken open. Before you can taste the sweetness of a ripe orange, you must first break open the peel. We all know these things are true but it's hard to thank God for the brokenness when we feel our lives sinking in the muddy river. But it's the brokenness that drives us back to God.

When your life seems to be going well . . . all your bills are paid, your family's healthy, you've got a nice home and a nice car, you're making a good salary . . . how's your prayer life?

We can all admit that when things are going well, we usually aren't as fervent in our prayer life as we need to be. When things are going well we should be thanking God for His abundant blessing in our life, but that usually doesn't happen, does it?

But let calamity come into our life in some form or another and we get pretty good at praying all of a sudden! We wear out the knees in our pants from all the kneeling and praying and crying out to God! And there's nothing at all wrong with that. God knows us better than we know ourselves, and sometimes we just have to learn our dependence on Him the hard way.

My friend, it's just a fact of the Kingdom that God will do whatever it takes to get to your heart. If we are selfish and hold on to things, trying too hard to fix our own messes or even ignore them altogether, He will lovingly and gently bring us to that place where our ax breaks. Well, maybe not always that gently! But He will get us to that place where we acknowledge that our true significance lies only in Him because on our own, we have nothing.

God's Solution Is Always the Stick!

Many people live their whole lives in brokenness. They are content to swing a broken ax, ignoring the fact that they're no longer being effective; they're no longer cutting down a tree, they're just going through the motions. In their denial, they continue to try to move ahead as if nothing ever happened. And because of that, they're never able to come to a complete understanding of their true destiny, their significance.

Others will recognize the brokenness in their life but never turn to God for help. They cast about trying one solution after another thinking they'll be able to fix their brokenness on their own. They might try to turn to other people and form unhealthy, co-dependent relationships in hopes that others will be able to do what only God can do.

Many turn to things as a vain attempt to fix their broken lives. Some turn to drugs, or alcohol, or sex, or food, or gambling, or any number of other things in hopes that they'll provide a solution. But all those things do is mask the pain. At best these things become a failed coping mechanism. At worst they are addictions that only serve to cause more pain, more dysfunction, and even more brokenness.

Either way, these people find themselves and their lives mired in the murky, muddy river bottom of despair. They can't see, they can't feel, they can't move, they can't even think. They just lay there mired in their brokenness until they're willing to admit to themselves that their life is broken, or they stop trying to fix it all by themselves and they finally cry out to God.

God answers with His "stick," which is the Cross of Christ and it's that cross that causes the miracle. The ax head floats, the problem that has been plaguing them for years comes to the surface of a murky life and is able to be dealt with once and for all.

My friend, everybody has a wiggly ax head. Everybody is going to come to that crisis moment at some point in their lives. It's the way of things when you live in a broken world like we do. If you think about it, without the crisis of the broken ax, that story wouldn't even be in the Bible. Without the broken ax head, it's just a nice story about a guy who joined some other guys on a building project. Nothing miraculous happens until the ax breaks, the man cries out, and Elisha throws the stick in the river.

I love this story. I love what this story can teach us. I love the picture of God using a stick to draw that ax head to the surface to be recovered and dealt with. Whenever I've preached this message before, I like to bring a bag or a pail of sticks with me up onto the platform. Of course, folks are curious as to why I have a pail of sticks with me. And just to keep the suspense going I don't say a word about the sticks or even acknowledge them until the very end of the message.

Then I ask, "Are you broken today? Do you need a stick in your life? If so, I want you to come down front and we're going to pray together and you're going to take a stick with you. This plain old stick will be a reminder to you that God cast a stick into the midst of your brokenness and brought forth a miracle. And that miracle is your healing, your wholeness, your purpose, and your destiny."

God's solution to your problem is a stick . . . the Cross of Christ. It's only the Cross of Christ that can heal your brokenness and bring you the fulfill-ment and significance and purpose you so desperately desire.

15

Within Reach— How God Helps Us Help Ourselves

Throughout the pages of this book we've followed the story of a man, a man who wanted to be noticed, he wanted to be picked to be a part of a cause, a cause that was bigger than he was. And once he was chosen, he had to borrow an ax in order to help, but there was a problem. The ax had a wiggly ax head and it broke right when the man was cutting down a tree. The ax head flew off and sunk in the depths of the murky river. But the man cried out to the prophet Elisha, "Alas, master! for it was borrowed." And the prophet cut a stick and threw it into the river right where the ax head went in.

And then a miracle occurred. I love the poetic wording in the *King James Version*, "And the man of God said, Where fell it? And he shewed him the place. And he cut down a stick, and cast it in thither; and the iron did swim" (2 Kings 6:6).

" . . . and the iron did swim."

What a miracle that must've been! God, in His mercy, caused the iron ax head to float. And not just float. God brought that iron ax head within reach so the man could pull it out of the river on his own. That way he could deal with his problem. That's the way God utilizes the sacrifice of His Son Jesus

Christ. He uses the cross to draw out the ax head, which represents our problem, our potential, and our purpose. He not only causes these things to float, He draws them all within reach.

I've mentioned that most everybody in the world is broken in some way or another. Everyone has come to that place where the ax head has flown off their ax handle and landed in the river and sunk to the muddy bottom. The fact is, most all of us have things lying at the bottom of our souls. Maybe you have a deep wound, a hurt from the past, an abuse from childhood that you've pushed down and tried to forget. Or maybe it's a traumatic event that took place in your life. Now it's just lying there, weighing on your soul, keeping you from your potential and your purpose in Christ. Not only that, it's keeping you from putting your stamp on this world and causing the ripple in eternity, living a life of significance that stretches to the generations beyond.

Maybe you've got something that's not been dealt with in your life and now it's buried down deep in the mud of your soul. So deep, you may not even remember that it's there. And as much as you might have tried to ignore it or push it down even deeper, it's come to define the person you've become.

Success Versus Fulfillment

Let me give you an example of what I'm talking about. One Sunday, I had a lawyer come down front to the altar after the sermon. Through tears, she opened up and told me her story. Her daddy had abused her mentally and emotionally all throughout her growing up years. He'd constantly beat her down with words like, "You'll never amount to anything. You're worthless." It broke my heart to hear her say those words and to imagine how hurtful they were to her.

Gently, I put my hand on her shoulder and asked her, "Did you know that the power of the Cross of Christ can draw that pain out of your heart? You can have a better life than what you're living right now."

This woman was wildly successful. She was one of the top lawyers in our city. This woman was so good that she didn't even need to advertise. She had more clients than she could handle, all coming to her because of her reputation for success in the courtroom. And her success through the years had brought her great wealth.

But ever since she was a child, she was driven to succeed by the hatred for her father that was hidden deep in her heart. Her wounds had given her the strength to be the top of her class in high school, the top of her class in college, the top of her class in law school, and now she was the top-practicing attorney in the whole metropolitan area, and all of it fueled by the hatred in her heart.

You know, you can glean strength from just about anything but she got her strength from the hatred for her father that developed in her heart because of the abuse she suffered all those years. But I told her, "You can find the better strength and live a fulfilled life, not just one where you make a lot of money. You realize, don't you, that a fulfilling life is much different than a successful life, right?"

I explained, "Success is just a scoreboard. It means you've won; you've come out on top. But fulfillment is something much deeper. You can achieve success and never feel fulfilled. Fulfillment is the feeling you get from walking in your destiny doing things that matter, things that will count for eternity. It's achieving the purpose for which you've been put on this earth. You can have that. All you need to do is allow the Cross of Christ to draw out that poison that's deeply mired down in the bottom of your soul. How about if you'd let me pray for you right now?"

But she couldn't let go of that hatred. She'd lived with the hatred so long; she couldn't imagine her life without it. She continued to hold on as she stood up and walked away from the altar that day. She never came back. My heart bled for her that day and continues to bleed for her as I write this today. I wept for her because I knew that her life could've been so much better if she could've let go of the hatred and allowed God to heal her heart.

Of course, she will remain wildly successful in this world but the ripple that her life will cause won't go much farther than just her. Her life will never be able to affect the generations to come.

It's the Supernatural that Makes the Difference

Pulling the ax head out of the mud and causing it to float within reach is a supernatural thing, it's a miracle that only God can do. What does it take to make a piece of metal float? Can you throw an ax head in your pool and make it come back up to the surface? Of course not. But God can. He's the God of the supernatural. And it's the experience of the supernatural in our life through the sacrifice of the Cross of Christ that will change not only your life; it'll change the world.

I think it's interesting that God supernaturally caused the piece of metal to float on the water, to swim up and float. Think about it, if God did that, He could've done anything with it. He could've caused it to fly out of the water and even land right back on the ax handle if He'd wanted to. But He didn't. It was important to God that the man reach in himself and pull that ax head out of the water.

Scripture never says but I'd like to think that once God restored the man's ax head that it fit perfectly on the ax handle. It was no longer wiggly. It was like new and the man could begin to swing with confidence. The handle was steady, the ax head was secure, and the blade was sharp. He was a whole new worker, working with a whole new purpose.

When he first started working, he was working with a wiggly ax head. His confidence was not high at all. He was swinging tentatively, knowing that the ax head could come off at any time. I imagine him saying to himself between swings, "This thing is going to come off. I'm not going to be able to keep working. I really want to be a part of this cause. I know for certain that this is what I'm supposed to be doing. But I don't know how I'm going to handle this wiggly ax head."

But now the problem has been dealt with and solved. He can reach his full potential. He can fulfill his purpose with confidence and swing that ax with all his might.

But without the supernatural miracle happening he would have no significance. And the truth is, neither do we. With no supernatural intervention from God it's all over. It's done. We have nothing and we will be nothing. We will accomplish nothing. We're nobody without God's miracle in our life.

Without Him, nothing else really matters. Nothing matters because it's all broken. It's all gone. But when God supernaturally brings our brokenness within reach so we can deal with it once and for all, we are fully and finally redeemed. You see, brokenness is the gateway to true significance.

In fact, if you've never experienced brokenness, you'll never experience true significance. It's just like a horse that is not broken is a horse that you cannot use. That horse may be beautiful and strong and fast but none of that matters because he hasn't yielded his will to the authority. We say that the horse has to be "broken." In other words, he has to learn to submit his will to the will of the master. We're the same way. It's the brokenness we experience in our lives that opens the door to the cross, which ultimately saves us and makes us whole.

Mad Dog Comes to Church

Living life with a broken ax is tough going. It's harder and not as effective or efficient. And the bad thing about brokenness is that it can even lead to even more brokenness. It can perpetuate itself until our lives are truly shattered and we're no longer able to even come close to accomplishing the purposes of God.

I had a fellow come to my church one time. His stepdaughter and her husband had actually come first and after the service they came down to the altar and got saved. The stepdaughter kept after her mom and stepdad to come and finally they agreed.

I want to tell you, this guy was rough. The first Sunday they came, they walked all the way down the center aisle and sat on the very front row, right in front of me. Now even though he lived in the city at the time, he was a rough old character from deep in the hills. He came into church on that first Sunday dressed in his faded bib overalls and the whole time I preached, he just sat there with his arms folded and a scowl on his face, all contorted. It was tough for me to concentrate on what I was preaching with this guy on the front row glaring at me. He looked like if he could've picked up a gun and shot me, I think he would have done it! It was unnerving!

He came back the next week and he was back on the front row with his overalls on, his arms folded tight across his chest and the angry scowl plastered on his face. I thought that at any moment he was going to get up out of his chair and walk up to me and snap my neck.

Then he came back a third week, not only on Sunday morning but he and his wife came Sunday night too. Then, to my surprise, they even came to the service on Wednesday night. Before the service began that night, he came up to me and through gritted teeth, he said, "I want to talk to you." I swallowed hard and stammered, "Uh . . . well . . . uh . . . okay . . . . " He said, "After church." I said, "All right" and the man shuffled off to his seat on the front row. I'm sure my sermon that night wasn't as good as it could have been because I was dreading the whole time what this guy wanted to talk to me about!

After the service, one of my lead ushers approached me and said, "Are you sure you want to meet with that guy? Do you know who he is?" Well, of course I didn't. He said, "Everyone calls him 'Mad Dog.'" And he proceeded to tell me just how crazy this guy was. He said, "Mad Dog's been known to pull up in his car to a red light and if someone just looks over at him wrong, he'll get out of his car and beat him to a pulp right there in the street! He's been jailed dozens of times because of his bad temper. He's as mean as a snake and he's been kicked out of almost every bar in town!"

Believe me, that's not what I wanted to hear just before sitting down to meet with him! My mouth was parched but I went up and told him I was ready to talk. He said, "I don't want to talk here. I want to go somewhere private." What I really wanted to do was just talk right there at the front of the church. I was thinking there was safety in numbers. But he wanted to go across the street and talk in the privacy of our church offices. So I relented and we started off to leave the building.

As we were walking out of the worship center my thoughts were racing, *Lord, I really don't want to have to talk to this man in private! Please help me!* Of course I was looking all around for my ushers, friends, or family . . . anyone who might see me leaving the building with this guy. But not one of them was even looking my way. I was thinking, *Come on, guys, do your job! Help me out over here!*

So we're walking across the street and I offer up a quick prayer, "Okay, God. You're going to have to help me out tonight. I have no idea what's going to happen here." I was really very nervous. I didn't know what this guy was thinking and hadn't a clue what he might do. We got over to my small office and the man and his wife sat in the chairs in front of my desk. I didn't want the desk to separate us so I pulled my chair out from around the desk and we formed a little circle around the coffee table.

I took a deep breath and looked at him. He had that same mean snarl of a face and he said to me, "I'm mad at God." Just like that. No preamble or easing into the conversation. He was just out with it. Well, l must have been pushed by the power of the Holy Spirit because I couldn't believe what I did next.

Before I even realized what I was doing, I jumped out of my seat and stepped over to him and pointed my finger in his chest and said, "You have no right to be mad at God." At once I realized what I was doing . . . I was pointing my finger at Mad Dog! I quickly retracted my finger and said, "Sorry about that" and I sat back down in my chair.

Now, years later, I know exactly what was going on. Like the attorney I mentioned earlier, this man had hatred and pain buried deep in the mud of his soul that needed to be dealt with. His ax head was broken. And for the last few weeks he'd been coming to church and hearing the message of the Gospel, it was the Cross of Christ that was gradually drawing the poison of that hatred out of his heart.

The Giant Man Breaks

In that moment, his face broke. That mean contorted look softened and his lower lip began to quiver. Hot tears pushed out of the corner of his eyes and traced down his cheek. He opened his mouth and said, "You're right. I have no right to be mad at God." I asked him, "What are you so mad about?"

Through many tears he told me the saddest story. He said, "The pride of my life and the joy of my heart was my little boy. He followed me everywhere and always wanted to be just like me. No matter where I went he wanted to be right there by my side. I had a hard time trying to get him to go to school because he just wanted to spend his whole day with me, riding around in my truck." He wiped a tear from his eye with the back of his hand and continued. "There's nothing on earth that brought me more joy than my little boy. And then one day, they called me and told me to get home, that there'd been an accident. I frantically raced home and found out that an accident had happened and my boy had died." As his wife quietly sobbed into her tissue, he continued, "I picked my boy up and rushed him to the hospital but it was too late. There was nothing they could do.

"When it came time for the funeral I didn't let anyone serve as a pall-bearer." Mad Dog was a big strapping man. He said, "I picked up my boy's little casket and put it up on my shoulder and carried him to his grave. Then I took the shovel and threw the first dirt on his grave. In fact, I wouldn't let anyone else bury him. I dismissed the gravediggers, telling them, 'I'll do it.' With every shovel full of dirt I threw in the grave I said, 'I hate You, God. I hate You. Why would You do this?' And for the last twenty years, I've hated every father that's had a son and every son that's had a father. I've hated everybody and everything." He broke down and sobbed into his hands, "I'm just so tired of hating." His wife reached over and patted his huge shoulder trying to ease his pain.

Once he'd recovered a bit he looked up at me and said, "Now don't be surprised if maybe Sunday morning I show up at the altar asking for prayer. I don't even know what that is but it seems like maybe something I need to do." I gently smiled and told him, "Ed, you know, we don't have to wait for Sunday. We can pray right now." He looked surprised, "We could?" "Yeah," I said, "we can pray right here, right now."

So we kneeled around my little coffee table and used it as an altar. I started to pray but he interrupted me saying, "What should I say?" I said, "Well, why don't you start by telling God that you hate Him and that you're mad at Him." He said, "I can say that to Him? I can tell Him I'm mad?" "Sure you can, Ed. It's no surprise to Him."

So he began to tell God exactly how he'd felt all those years. He started out tentatively but then picked up steam. He started beating down on that coffee table with his massive fists. He cried out, "God, I've hated You. I've hated everybody. My life has been hell on earth and I've lived like hell."

He said, "I don't know all about it but I'm asking You to come into my heart. I'm asking You to help me." I whispered, "Ask Him in His Son's name to forgive you." And he said, "In Jesus' name, please forgive me."

All at once his face lit up and a big smile stretched across his face. He looked at me and he said, "He did it." I asked, "He did what?" He said, "It's gone." I asked, "What's gone?" Through tears of joy he said, "All the hate. He forgave me. He did it." His wife raised her hands and began to praise God. She knew that God had done a miracle in her man.

The Redeeming Power of the Stick

Dear reader, that's the power of the stick. The Cross of Christ had pulled out of him all that poison, all that hatred he'd carried around for years. Eventually Mad Dog became one of our ushers. Some Sundays he could hardly "ush" because he'd get so shoutin' happy! He'd rub his big hands together and let out a whoop that sounded like an old train whistle. He'd run around the church shouting. Make no mistake, he was still Mad

Dog . . . but he was our Mad Dog. And ever since that prayer he was crazy over something a lot better.

I remember the day he died I'd gone to visit him. I patted his cold marble face and bent down and whispered in his ear, "Ed, hold your little boy. Cradle him in your arms forever. Because the power of the cross gives you a destiny here and a hope later." And God threw the stick and it drew out the life from his body and Mad Dog peacefully went to be with the Lord.

Listen, I know the power of counseling. I know the benefit of twelve-step programs. But there are some things that are mired so deeply in the mud of our souls that nothing can work except the Cross of Christ. Nothing can heal like He can heal. Nothing can deliver like He can deliver. Nothing can save like He can save.

Without the Cross of Christ old Mad Dog would've died with that poison hatred still lodged deep in his heart. He wouldn't have been able to fulfill anything in this life but for the Cross of Christ. God used the cross to bring his hate up out of the mud and within reach so he could deal with it. I remember the last time he heard me preach. He came up to me afterwards and said, "Oh, preacher. I'm so thankful for what God has done for me."

God cut the stick and the iron did swim. Supernaturally. I pray that you can experience the supernatural presence of God Himself in your life. We all have things buried in our souls that only the stick can resolve. At the end of the day, there's something lying at the bottom of your heart that only the supernatural is going to be able to heal.

Your ax head is floating. It's right there on the surface. Now it's up to you to grab on to it.

Conclusion
Grab the Ax Head—Finding Your Significance

We started this book by talking about a walk in the woods where I saw three words crudely carved into a tree, "I was here." To me, that is the deep cry of the human heart, to be recognized, to find true significance. You see this play out all throughout our culture today, people searching for purpose. Crying out for destiny.

We read the story from 2 Kings 6 where a man . . . just like the man who carved those words in that tree, wanted to find significance when he happened upon the prophets in the middle of a building project. He knew immediately that he wanted to be a part of this cause. He didn't require his name to be trumpeted from the rooftops; he was happy to work in anonymity.

He just wanted to be a part. He wanted to be chosen, chosen for a cause that was bigger than he was. He wanted to be part of something big, something that would reach distant generations, with an impact in the eternal. And he was chosen . . . but he had no tools to work with. He needed an ax.

He was able to borrow an ax but it had a wiggly ax head. It wasn't whole but it was his and he began to work in earnest. He was feeling good. He'd been chosen to be a part of the project and he was chopping wood, making a difference until all at once . . .

His ax head flew off the handle and sailed into the murky river. Suddenly he cried out for help. He didn't ignore the problem or try to solve it on his own. He cried out immediately, "Alas, master! for it was borrowed."

The master (Elisha) asked where the ax head landed and the man pointed to the spot. Then Elisha cut a stick and threw it in the spot where the ax head landed. And the iron did swim. The ax head began to float. It simply came to the surface and floated over within reach so the man could easily pick it up out of the water and place it back on the ax handle.

At that point, I believe, the man went back to work. Scripture is silent on the subject but I believe the man went back to work chopping that tree with renewed vigor. His ax head wasn't wiggly anymore. It was tightly fastened to the handle with a gleaming sharp edge. He was able to swing with confidence, knowing that the ax would do its job without breaking.

Your Ax Head Is Right There Within Reach

Friend, when you cry out for help from God, He's right there. He cuts a stick, which is the Cross of Christ and He tosses it toward your problem. Like a poultice draws poison from a wound, the stick draws the iron from the muddy depths and brings it within reach so you can deal with it.

Maybe your ax head has been buried down deep in the muddy bottom of that river for a very long time. When it finally emerges from the depths, it's going to be grimy and gross. You may take one look at it and think, "There's no way I want to grab onto that. It's too nasty."

Believe me, I've seen hatred and pride, resentment and bitterness, hopelessness and despair when it's been mired in blackness for many years. It's not a pretty sight. Think of a wound that's bound up without cleaning it out first. The wound might heal over but infection will develop and cause all kinds of problems. The only way to treat that infection is to open up the wound again and clean all that nastiness out.

Some people put off the procedure because they don't want to go through all that pain again. But the only way to really deal with the wound is to go back in and get that infection taken care of.

The same is true here. You have to pick up that nasty ax head yourself. You have to deal with the problem that God has brought to the surface. You are the only one who can do this, no one else. Even God won't do this for you. He's already done His part; He's revealed the problem. Now this part is for you only. All you need is the courage to reach out and take it for yourself.

Reach Out and Own It!

It's all up to you now. No one else. You've worked hard trying to be a part of some great cause. But your ax head has broken and sailed off into the river. I want you to stop ignoring the fact that your ax head has broken. It's time to recognize your brokenness.

Now once you've recognized and admitted to your brokenness, cry out for help. Stop trying to fix things yourself. This is something you cannot fix on your own. We're all broken in some way and we all need a Savior. Cry out to Him.

Now, as you've cried out to Him, ask Him to pass the cross of His precious Son's sacrifice over your life and draw out the poison, the thing that is keeping you from discovering your significance in this life.

What is He showing you? Do you see Hatred or Fear rising to the surface of your heart? Is it Unforgiveness floating near the shore? Whatever it is, I want you to mentally grab it up and own it. No matter how muddy and gross it might be, I want you to take it up and allow the Lord to clean it up, repair it. Make it like new. Let Him transform your Fear into Faith, your Despair into Hope, your Grief into Joy, and your Hatred into Love.

Do you know what your broken ax head is? Maybe you've searched for purpose and significance for years and never known what's holding you back. You know you aren't whole but you've never known just what the problem is. I ask that God reveal that to you now by the power of the Holy Spirit.

Or maybe you know exactly what your broken ax head is. Chances are you've known for years but you've lacked the courage to take it up and deal with it. Now here's your chance. You can see the ax head right there, floating on the surface of your heart. Now is the time to take it up.

Your significance is right there. Can you see it?

God gave you this one life to live. Now it's up to you to reach out and grab it!

You are significant! You are living a life of purpose!

Author Contact

If you would like to contact Troy Ervin, find out more information, purchase books, or request him to speak, please contact:

Troy P. Ervin
701 Chamber Drive
Milford, Ohio 45150
513-735-2555
www.troyervinministries.com
info@troyervinministries.com

Follow Troy Ervin!
www.facebook.com/PastorTroyErvin
www.instagram.com/troyervinministries
www.twitter.com/ervin_troy